BUSINESS LAW

GRID SERIES IN LAW

Consulting Editor
THOMAS W. DUNFEE, The Wharton School, University of Pennsylvania
Atteberry, Pearson & Litka, *Real Estate Law,* Second Edition
Dunfee, Gibson, Lamber & McCarty, *Modern Business Law*
Dunfee & Gibson, *Modern Business Law: An Introduction to Government and Business,* Second Edition
Dunfee, Gibson, Lamber & McCarty, *Modern Business Law: An Introduction to the Legal Environment of Business*
Dunfee, Gibson & McCarty, *Modern Business Law: Contracts*
Dunfee & Reitzel, eds., *Business Law: Key Issues and Concepts*
Erickson, Dunfee & Gibson, *Antitrust and Trade Regulation: Cases and Materials*
Francois, *Mass Media Law and Regulation,* Second Edition
Litka, *Business Law,* Second Edition
Litka & Inman, *The Legal Environment of Business: Text, Cases, and Readings*
Stern & Yaney, *Cases in Labor Law*
Wolfe & Naffziger, *Legal Perspectives of American Business Associations*

OTHER BOOKS IN THE GRID SERIES IN LAW

Naffziger & Knauss, *Basic Guide to Federal Labor Law*

BUSINESS LAW
Key Issues and Concepts

Edited by
Thomas W. Dunfee
The Wharton School
University of Pennsylvania

J. David Reitzel
Graduate School of Financial Sciences
The American College

Grid Publishing, Inc., Columbus, Ohio

Library of Congress Cataloging in Publication Data
Main entry under title:

Business law.

  (Grid series in law)
  1. Commercial law—United States. I. Dunfee, Thomas W. II. Reitzel, J. David.
KF889.B84   346'.73'07   78-17091
ISBN O-88244-177-9

CONTENTS

PART III: BUSINESS LAW

Preface

Business and collegiate law instructors teaching an introductory course often face a problem of how to bring current developments and supplemental issues into their courses. Many use supplemental class handouts of cases and journal article copies.

This book is designed as a supplemental text. The topics covered either go beyond those typically dealt with in the basic business law texts or involve recent significant developments. The price has been held low so that it can be used in conjunction with the basic full-sized text.

We have been excited throughout the developmental stage of this book by the idea of having many of the most prominent scholars and authors in our field write a short chapter on a favorite topic relevant to the basic law course. As the following pages indicate, our group of prominent, experienced authors responded admirably to the task. We thank them all for their efforts, patience, and promptness.

This book represents another of the diversified components of the Grid Series in Law. The inside front cover lists the ever increasing catalogue of collegiate law books. These books cover many different substantive topics and are designed for a variety of uses. We think *Key Issues and Concepts* is one of the most unique and interesting to appear in this field.

Part I

Legal System and Background

The Confucian Chinese subscribed to a principle of cosmic harmony. If that harmony was disturbed, it had to be restored. Criminal misconduct had a terribly jangling effect, and the restoration of cosmic harmony required the application of precisely graduated temporal punishments. Confucian authorities left much of the law unwritten, because they thought that would prevent cosmic disturbance. Written law, they thought, would cause people to become disputatious and to abandon the supreme goal of tranquility. Confucian philosophy directly affected the content and administration of Confucian law.

In Anglo-American law, underlying philosophies and other background matters are not so readily apparent. Yet, they exist, and attention to them can aid immeasureably in the study and understanding of our legal system. Part I of this book deals with some important aspects of American law.

Legal research is essential if people are to discover, interpret, or evaluate the law. In Chapter 1, Professor Reitzel discusses the nature and kinds of legal research, the relationship of legal research to nonlegal research, some uses which nonlawyers might make of legal research and writing, and some techniques for judging the quality of legal research and writing.

In a general way, Professor Tucker in Chapter 2 discusses philosophy and law. He focuses on how the concepts of motive, fairness, and good faith have been used as tests of lawful conduct. By drawing on illustrations from a wide range of business litigation, Professor Tucker demonstrates that motive, fairness, and good faith have a firm place in American jurisprudence.

In Chapter 3, Professor Fisher comments on the relationship between legal philosophy and the Uniform Commercial Code. First, he summarizes the main tenets of the major schools of legal thought. Then, by discussing specific sections or rules of the Code, he illustrates its jurisprudential implications.

Part I

Legal System and Background

Legal Research—Nature, Methods, and Applications

J. David Reitzel*

Law students of all levels may find themselves faced with a bewildering array of legal materials.[1] For business law students, the problem can be particularly acute, because a principal aim of most business law courses is to present a rather wide spectrum of law and to reveal its relationship to business and society, all in an amazingly short period of time. Legal research will be mentioned, but the major emphasis of a business law course is likely to be the products rather than the process of legal research.

Yet, preliminary attention to the nature of legal research can produce a number of short-term and long-term benefits. A student who knows the nature and kinds of legal research will gain interpretive insight into the many legal materials being studied. This insight may be helpful in judging the propriety of law which has been or is about to be enacted. Background in legal research will also enable students to develop criteria by which later to evaluate the work of lawyers and other business consultants. And, of course, knowledge of legal research tends to round out one's knowledge of research in general.

THE NATURE OF LEGAL RESEARCH

Many people perceive legal research as a lawyer's library search for a legal precedent, a search which is mechanistically determined by the doctrine of *stare decisis* and which is therefore (and for other reasons) utterly unscientific. This perception is inaccurate in at least two major respects. First, legal research is not restricted to lawyers. Scholars, judges, and other engage in it, for a variety of purposes. Second, legal research, properly conducted, is far from

*Chairman, Department of Business Law. The American College.

mechanistic. A search for precedent (broadly defined here to include judicial and administrative decisions) is only one of the investigations called for by the doctrine of *stare decisis*. The doctrine also requires attention to whether the precedents are in harmony with contemporary social needs. Indeed, there may be no precedent. In such a situation, the resolution of a legal problem may require investigation of tangential, nonprecedential law if any exists.

Nevertheless, lawyers need tactical knowledge of precedents and their social underpinnings; lawyers may be called upon to decide whether to retain or to reject a precedent; or a scholar may wish to examine how, why or to what extent a precedent has become established. Whatever the reason for examining precedents, legal researchers explore not only judicial decisions and other rules of law such as statutes, but also the nature of the thing being regulated and the views of the lawmakers regarding the nature of that thing. In conducting their explorations and in dealing with the legal uncertainty which arises from conflicting law, gaps in the law, and shifting lines of policy, legal researchers engage in thought processes which are similar to the thought processes involved in nonlegal research. Precisely how a given piece of legal research fits into the spectrum of legal and nonlegal research depends upon the legal researcher's goal or point of view, and upon the level of sophistication required for the research.

Many people distinguish between "applied" research and "basic" or "pure" research. Applied research is concerned with the solution of real-life problems that normally require someone to make an action or policy decision. Pure research aims at expanding the frontiers of knowledge and does not directly involve pragmatic problems. The pure research investigator uses his results to decide how acceptable a given theory is.[2] Yet, despite differences between the applied and pure varieties, research has been defined broadly as any organized inquiry designed and carried out to provide information for solving a problem.[3] All legal research falls within this broad definition. Most legal research is properly characterized as applied research (research designed to enable someone to make an action or policy decision). Some legal research may approach, contribute substantially to, or constitute pure research (research which expands the frontiers of knowledge by testing a theory).

Like research in general, legal research has a variety of types. Much legal research is concerned with the legal system itself, in historical, descriptive, analytical, or comparative terms. The topic of discussion in this chapter is another kind of legal research, an investigation of the law for the purpose of resolving a legal problem or determining the characteristics of the law. The most typical legal researchers are lawyers, judges, drafters of legislation, personnel employed by administrative agencies, and law professors; but the list could include law students, nonlegal scholars, and others. Legal research should not be confused with the uses to which the research may be put. Legal research is a process of investigation and problem-solving. A brief which a lawyer presents in court is based upon the lawyer's research, but the brief is essentially the lawyer's argumentation in which he presents a legal position most favorable to his client—more favorable, perhaps, than the lawyer's investigation of the client's situation would warrant. Four kinds of legal researchers are discussed: the lawyer-advocate, the judge, the drafter of legislation, and the scholar.[4]

THE LAWYER-ADVOCATE'S RESEARCH

The lawyer-advocate (hereafter called lawyer) may be hired to work within the constraints of existing rules. If a client has need for an ordinary corporate structure, and if the rules of incorporation are clear, the lawyer may need to investigate the corporate law only to learn the legal mechanics of incorporation. Much legal research is intended to unearth uncontroversial legal requirements and thus may be termed descriptive. However, the fact that the investigation of the law is straightforward does not mean that the total research task is simple, for the lawyer must determine that the client's situation is indeed routine and the legal rules clear.

Frequently, lawyers are required by their clients' needs to test the limits of existing rules or to encourage the creation of new ones. If a client wishes to accomplish an unusual purpose with a corporate structure, or if he wishes to set up an unusually complex corporation, the lawyer may need to focus his research on unexplored or ambiguous aspects of corporate law. To the task of analyzing the client's situation is added the task of wrestling with the uncertainty of law and predicting which course of action will serve the client's interest. Where the lawyer confronts uncertainty of law, his research will begin to exhibit the characteristics of formal nonlegal research. That is, data (the law and gaps in the law) will be assessed, and hypotheses (*e.g.*, that the client's plan is legally feasible) will be accepted or rejected.

The lawyer's function as an advocate shapes the lawyer's research in two principal ways. Because a lawyer must serve the client's interest, the research will be problem oriented (applied) and particularistic. The lawyer will not search for universal truths unless the client's interest calls for such a search.

A more fundamental impact of the advocacy function becomes clear where the lawyer fashions an argument or other plan for the client. Where argumentation is called for, the lawyer's investigation of the law might occur in two stages (although the lawyer might not be conscious of two distinct stages). First, the lawyer must discover what the law says about the client's situation. To conduct a sound investigation of the law affecting the client, the lawyer must assess the unfavorable law as well as the favorable. This first stage of research might be termed the "objective" stage, because to make a sound assessment, the lawyer must put aside any bias for or against the client. Then, after a clear-eyed assessment of the law (and the facts), the lawyer will be in a position to engage in any "advocacy" research that might be needed. If the initial investigation reveals that the law favors the client, there will be little or no need for further exploration of the law. If the law is unfavorable to the client, the advocacy phase will be aimed at finding or creating a legal theory more favorable to the client, or at weakening arguments unfavorable to the client. If the law says nothing directly applicable to the client's problem, the advocacy phase of the research will be aimed at creating a favorable solution by way of analogy from any applicable tangential law. Since the advocacy phase of a lawyer's research is the most obvious to the public, many people view lawyers as unobjective and therefore as incapable of true research. Yet, the strict objectivity which supposedly characterizes scientific research also typifies the initial stages of a competent lawyer's research and enhances his chances for success as an advocate.

4

THE JUDGE'S RESEARCH

A judge's function and viewpoint differ considerably from those of a lawyer, and the difference affects the content of the judge's legal research and his examination of lawyers' briefs. A judge's function is to decide cases and controversies in a manner permitted by the law of evidence and procedure. Whether the judge is called upon to resolve a dispute where the law is clear, to resolve an ambiguity in a statute, to render a decision (make law) where no substantive law exists, or to decide a question of evidence or procedure, the judge must decide which line of argument, if any, to accept. In making such decisions, the judge is expected to be impartial and objective; to recognize and cope with the professional partiality of lawyers; and, where possible, to adopt a legal position which tends to preserve the usefulness of the law and the legal system for future generations. The judge's research will therefore tend toward neutrality, independence, and objectivity.[5] Since a judge deals with narrowly framed disputes, the judge's research is as "applied" and can be as particularistic as a lawyer's. But since the judge must consider the consequences of his decision as precedent upon the substance and procedures of the law, judicial research into the law may have overtones of universality not found in a lawyer's brief.

THE LEGISLATOR'S RESEARCH

A third category of legal researcher is the drafter of legislation. The legal research associated with legislative drafting should be distinguished from the legislature's factual investigation of the need for a law or the acceptability of a proposed law. A factual investigation of need (or consequences) might be conducted by committees of the legislature, by staff members or individual legislators, by the author of a proposed law, or by others interested in the proposal.[6] In contrast, legal research underlying a proposed law is primarily for the benefit of the author in drafting the proposal, although persons other than the author might conduct legal research for the purpose of checking the legal soundness of the proposal, or for the purpose of offering an amendment.

Many factors determine the nature of the legal research underlying proposed legislation. The development of a simple amendment to a straightforward statute might require little or no investigation of the law. The development of major tax legislation, on the other hand, could require a thorough investigation of the technical aspects of tax law, and of the economic and social implications of the existing and the proposed law.

Complexity of research aside, the function or viewpoint of a person who drafts legislation affects the nature of the drafter's legal research. Many proposals for legislation come from special interest groups seeking advantage for themselves. Authors of such proposals are advocates for the groups, and the underlying legal research will resemble the research of a lawyer-advocate. Even a proposal for a law intended to benefit the public generally is likely to require advocacy research so that the author may meet at least the legal objections of any groups affected adversely. And, since legislation is essentially prospective and general in its application (in contrast with the typically retro-spective and particularistic activities of the lawyer and the judge), the legal researcher-drafter often acquires the role of sociolegal planner whose work may affect millions of people. Consequently, a drafter's legal research might be expected to focus on the socioeconomic functions of the existing and the proposed law. The drafters of the Uniform Commercial Code, for example, took such matters into account as they devised rules for the conduct of com-mercial transactions.

THE SCHOLAR'S RESEARCH

Many kinds of scholars investigate the law. A professor of education might look into the law affecting schools, for the purpose of describing or evaluating the rights and duties of school boards, teachers, and students. An economist might study the nature and economic consequences of the federal antitrust law. Anthropologists might look at primitive law for insights into life in primi-tive societies. The work of law professors, however, is more typical of the scholarly investigation of the law.

The research of law professors begins to depart from the applied research of the lawyer, the judge, and the drafter of legislation. A lawyer conducts what-ever investigation is necessary to resolve the problem of a client. The scope of the research can be quite narrow, focusing, for example, on such questions as whether a particular theory of law is available to the client. A law professor looking at the same problem is likely to take a broader view. His focus will be on whether that theory of law *should* be available to a particular type of client: What are the characteristics and consequences of that theory for that kind of client and for the population in general? Are other theories more suitable? Many lawyers raise such questions on behalf of their clients, but the scholar's research into the law is likely to be broader, more analytical, and less partial, often culminating in a proposal for a change in the law or in the administra-tion of the law.

Some legal scholars go beyond research into the law itself. Their intent may be, for example, to categorize the law or to reveal a general "truth" about the law, the legal system, or the social order of which the legal system is a part. How have the law and legal institutions shaped (or been shaped by) political, social, or economic processes? What are the implications for change? The answers to such fundamental questions require the most rigorous research into the nature of society as well as into the nature of the law. This kind of research often generates the kind of explanation and prediction characteristic of pure research.

What, then, are the principal functions of legal research? They may be sum-marized as follows:

1. To provide a lawyer with a basis upon which to advise a client in the conduct of the client's affairs.
2. To provide a judge with a basis for applying law to individuals and groups.

3. To provide a lawmaker (legislator, judge, or administrative agency) with a basis for modifying or terminating existing law or for developing new law.
4. To provide legal scholars and other scholars such as historians, sociologists, and anthropologists with legal information relevant to their descriptive, analytical, or other scholarly endeavors.

THE METHODS OF LEGAL RESEARCH

The methods and procedures of legal research are analogous to those of nonlegal research. Both kinds of research can be viewed as a problem-solving process involving four major stages: exploration of the situation, development of a research design, collection of data, and analysis and interpretation of data.[7] The paragraphs which follow describe in general terms how a lawyer might conduct research on behalf of a client. Other kinds of legal researchers would adapt this four-stage process to suit their peculiar research needs.

EXPLORATION OF THE SITUATION

The kind of preliminary exploration required of a lawyer depends on how well the client can describe the problem to be resolved. Often, the client can define clearly the legal task the lawyer is to accomplish: handle an adoption, prepare a will, develop an estate plan, set up a corporation, or represent the client in a criminal or civil action. Where the client can only describe a bothersome situation, he relies on the lawyer to characterize the legal problem. In any event, the lawyer must collect facts about the client's situation and assess the facts to determine whether the client's perception of the situation is accurate and to estimate the kind of legal help needed. The main purpose of the diagnostic, exploratory stage is to enable the lawyer to identify the legal issues—in essence, to formulate hypotheses and investigative questions.

DEVELOPMENT OF A RESEARCH DESIGN

After the lawyer has determined the nature of the legal problem, he will formulate a "research design," or a general plan for resolving the problem. The plan will address some or all of the following matters: the details of the client's needs, the law of the situation, the development of any proof that may be required, the nature and operation of the legal machinery that may be involved in resolving the problem, and potential means of settling a dispute out of court. If the lawyer is to prepare a document such as a contract or a will, the research plan will focus on how to draft a document which will fulfill the client's needs and yet withstand any subsequent litigation. If the lawyer is to represent the client before a governmental authority, the plan must take into account the nature of the hearing and rules of procedure and evidence. If the lawyer is to negotiate the settlement of a dispute between private parties, the plan must anticipate a variety of negotiatory techniques and their relationship to any litigation that might ensue. The precise content and form of the plan will depend, in other words, upon the nature of the client's problem.

COLLECTION OF DATA

A lawyer collects data from the time of the first interview with the client. The client's explanation of the problem might be the main source of information upon which the lawyer bases his diagnosis of the situation. As the legal research progresses beyond the exploratory stage, however, the lawyer may need more information about the facts and the law. For projects such as developing an estate plan, the lawyer will need detailed financial and other personal information about the client, his family, and his goals regarding the use and distribution of his property. An interview with the client could produce that kind of information, the analysis of which could lead the lawyer to a search for more information—for example, information about relative yields, safety, and liquidity of alternative forms of investment. If the client's problem is likely to require litigation, the lawyer will collect factual data for other purposes—to support the client's claim or to weaken the claim of the adversary. Finally, the lawyer may need to collect information about the law—what the substantive and procedural law is, how the law has been changed, social changes that might justify a departure from precedent, and so on.

In collecting information about the law, the lawyer utilizes primary, secondary, and tertiary reference material. *Primary* materials state the law. That is, they set out the actual authoritative statements of official decision makers such as judges and legislatures. Examples of primary (authoritative) materials are constitutions, treaties, acts of legislatures, opinions of courts, regulations of executive and administrative agencies, and city ordinances. *Secondary* materials, on the other hand, are unofficial explanations of or comments on the primary materials. Examples are legal treatises, legal encyclopedias, "restatements" of the law, and law journals. Secondary materials usually are prepared by legal scholars or expert legal practitioners. Although unofficial, such materials often are very persuasive to those who make or apply the law. Legal researchers find secondary materials helpful because of the perspective they lend to primary materials.[8] *Tertiary* materials are books of access to primary and secondary materials—indexes, digests, and other "finding aids." Since a lawyer is formally trained to locate, analyze, and interpret the law, the collection of legal data is probably the most consistently structured aspect of the lawyer's data gathering.

The gathering of non-law facts is quite another matter. A law student becomes acutely aware of the legal relevance of facts and the need for thorough preparation in confronting the factual aspects of a legal problem; but the collection of non-law facts is an expertise learned primarily on the job. Since most legal problems concern relatively nontechnical client activities, the methods of interview, personal observation, informal study, the informal consultation with knowledgeable persons often provide a sufficient factual basis for legal decision-making, especially where the lawyer's task does not involve litigation and the consequent proofmaking. Fact-finding in preparation for litigation can be much more exacting. A lawyer is not necessarily trained in the methods of empirical science, and he certainly is not trained in the spectrum of scientific specialities relevant to his client's problems. Yet, he may be called upon to deal with complex scientific issues such as the validity of a police radar reading, the toxic properties of a food additive, the effects of racial segregation on school children, the psychological nature of an accused murderer, the economic impacts of antitrust legislation, or the effects of industrial activities on the environment. If the lawyer lacks the relevant scientific knowledge, he must consult with experts or acquire the knowledge in some other way. Perhaps with the aid of consultants, the lawyer may need to utilize the statistical methods of data collection and data reporting characteristic of much empirical research.

ANALYSIS AND INTERPRETATION OF DATA

Emory defines analysis as "the breaking down and ordering of data into meaningful groups, plus the searching for patterns of relationship among these data groups." With regard to interpretation, he notes that it "involves the drawing of inferences and conclusions from the analyzed data. In one sense interpretation is concerned with relationships within the collected data, partially overlapping analysis. Interpretation also extends beyond the data of the study to include the results of other research, theory, and hypotheses."[9]

A lawyer routinely engages in the analysis and interpretation of law and facts. The processes may be conducted informally, as where the lawyer sorts relevant from irrelevant facts in order to characterize a client's situation as a particular kind of legal problem. Or the processes may be quite formal and complex, as where the lawyer develops proof according to the rules of evidence and procedure before a trier of fact. In some instances, a lawyer's practice requires him to become familiar with the analythical-interpretive methods of empirical science. Knowledge of those methods may be essential if a trial lawyer, for example, is to make an effective argumentation regarding group behavior, the extent of atmospheric contamination, or other matters involving sampling and the statistical analysis and interpretation of data.

A lawyer's research strength is his ability to analyze and interpret the law. As he develops a legal brief from a multitude of conflicting or tangential cases, statutes, and administrative rulings, he must anticipate myriad interpretive pitfalls. For example, statutes may be ambiguous or vague. The lawyer must know how to respond to ambiguity and vagueness, and the response may vary according to the kind of statute, the kind and degree of vagueness, the intention of the legislature in leaving the statute vague, and the constitutional permissibility of the vagueness. In assessing judicial opinions, the lawyer may need to distinguish the *holding* (statement of what is actually decided as well as statements logically necessary to support the holding) from *obiter dictum* (things said in passing which are not to have the weight of precedent). Where statute, holding, or administrative ruling is unclear, the lawyer may have to seek clarification in other law or in secondary materials, or resort to any applicable interpretive guidelines. Where specific bits of law are clear but conflicting, the lawyer must be prepared to rationalize inconsistencies. In any event, the lawyer must estimate the weight to be accorded each bit of law and must meet many other interpretive challenges.

EVALUATION OF LEGAL WRITING

Many forms of legal writing are available to the public and can be helpful in understanding a variety of socio-legal problems. The business applications of legal research provide an example. The law is an integral part of financial planning for individuals, labor-management relations, personnel policies, the protection of property rights of a business, avoiding infringements of the property rights of others, business financing, mergers, product pricing, advertising—in short, the gamut of business activities. A business manager's taking the law into account as a part of the planning process facilitates business activities. Similar action by consumers and others can provide similar benefits.

But how can a person untrained in law evaluate legal writing and thus reduce his chances of being misled? A first step would be to become familiar with the characteristics of sound legal writing. The characteristics vary according to the kind of writing attempted. Legal writing for uneducated consumers would differ from that intended for sophisticated professionals, and the evaluative criteria would differ.

Suppose that a person wished to evaluate the writing of a legal scholar. We might expect the scholar to refrain from a lawyer's argumentation and to present, instead, a balanced and objective legal analysis of a business or social problem. A legal writer who is attempting such an analysis should perform all of the following tasks relevant to the research situation:

1. *Goal clarification.* The writer should state and clarify as far as possible the objective which the law in question is or was intended to promote. The statement of legal purpose should reveal the interests sought to be protected by the law.
2. *Trend description.* The writer should factually describe how the particular law or line of decisions has evolved. The description will help the reader to see where the law has come from and how it has evolved, to relate the law to its social context, and to assess the value of the law as a means of accomplishing its intended objective.
3. *Analysis of conditioning factors.* The writer should explain any factors affecting the trend of the law. They include subjective factors influencing the decision-makers (legislators, judges, executives, administrators), and objective factors in the society (*e.g.,* custom, problems, change).
4. *Trend projection.* The writer's task is to predict where the law is heading, not just by simple extrapolation of past trends, but by taking into account anticipated conditioning factors.
5. *Consideration of alternatives.* In carrying out this critical and creative task, the writer states and evaluates alternatives to the projected trend in

the law. The writer may conduct his evaluation in light of the intended goals of the law, but he is free to recommend new goals as well as new law.

Having considered the legal writing in light of these characteristics,[10] its reader might wish to check the accuracy of key statements, keeping in mind the distinctions among primary, secondary, and tertiary references, and the distinction between holding and dictum. Knowledge of these evaluative matters does not assure that a layman will correctly interpret complex legal materials, but such knowledge does provide a frame of reference for identifying what the legal writer is attempting to do and, perhaps, what he is leaving out. If lawyers are to be involved in a situation, this frame of reference provides a basis for deciding what questions to ask them and for judging the quality of their work.

CONCLUSION

The thought processes required for legal research are not markedly different from those required for other kinds of research, although the objectives of legal research and the materials dealt with may be quite different. Much legal research is aimed at resolving legal disputes, facilitating business and non-business activities, discovering the nature of the law and its social context, and preserving the generality of the law while resolving individual cases. Because the social context of the law is inseparable from the law itself, legal research frequently involves a search for policy. Since policy is a matter of human judgment and is often unexpressed, the conclusions of a legal researcher may be tentative and inexact. Nevertheless, legal research has a methodology which encourages thoughtful investigation and permits the independent cross-checking characteristic of nonlegal research.

ENDNOTES

1. The author thanks Professor Thomas J. Holton, Seton Hall School of Law, for reviewing the manuscript for this chapter.
2. C.W. EMORY, BUSINESS RESEARCH METHODS 7 (1976).
3. Id. at 8.
4. Not all lawyers, judges and drafters of legislation conduct legal research for every problem they encounter. Lower court judges, for example, frequently rely on the briefs presented by opposing counsel and *amicus curiae*. High court judges are more likely to conduct or direct independent legal research, but do not always do so.
5. Judicial objectivity may mean nothing more than a suspension of bias in an attempt to detect aspects of the legal problem which the lawyers have failed to mention.
6. Whether the hearing conducted by a committee is a critical study preceding decision on the merits of the proposal is subject to serious doubt. More likely, a legislative hearing is used to marshal support for or against the proposal in furtherance of commitments already made, or is used to estimate the degree of political support for the proposal. Cohen, *Hearing on a Bill: Legislative Folklore?* 37 MINNESOTA LAW REVIEW 34 (1952).

7. For an overview and illustration of these four stages in a nonlegal research context, see Emory, *supra* note 2, at 65-73.

8. In nonlegal research, the words primary and secondary are used to describe data or sources of data. Phenomena directly observed by a researcher are "primary." Phenomena reported by others (*i.e.*, not directly observed by the researcher or originally gathered under his direction) are "secondary" and presumptively less reliable than primary data. Commentary or explanatory materials would not fall within the usual meaning of "data."

It is appropriate to categorize primary legal references as secondary sources of data, just as it is appropriate to categorize governmental compilations of data as secondary when they are used by a noncompiling, nonlegal researcher. However, the rationale of legal researchers for the primary-secondary distinction differs fundamentally from that of nonlegal researchers. In legal research, the distinction has much less to do with reliability than with "officialness." The distinction enables legal researchers to determine with some confidence which statements are binding and which are merely persuasive.

9. Emory, *supra* note 2, at 337.

10. The writer should also state his value premises and expressly reveal other factors (such as financial and professional alignments) affecting his objectivity. However, as desirable as such statements may be, making them is problematical. Few legal writers make them. For examples of such statements, see *Introduction* to J. HALL, THEFT, LAW AND SOCIETY at x, xii-xix (2d ed. 1952); J. HALL, GENERAL PRINCIPLES OF CRIMINAL LAW 2-5 (2d ed. 1960).

2

Motive, Fairness, and Good Faith

Edwin W. Tucker*

Legislation and administrative agency rules, as well as agency and court decisions, may assign rights and duties on the basis of motive, fairness or good faith. By paying attention to one of these three factors, the law comes to the assistance of parties who otherwise would be denied relief.

American law has traditionally recognized a broad liberty to contract. Severe legal restrictions on the ability of persons to enter into contract terms of their own choosing are obviously at odds with a laissez-faire, individual-oriented economic, political, and social order. In the late 1800's and early 1900's, under the judicially established doctrine of "substantive due process," the Supreme Court severely limited the power of government to place restrictions on the competency of persons to enter into binding agreements. For example, it struck down such laws as a statute which directed that persons not work more than a certain number of hours a week[1] and a statute barring an employer from requiring as a condition of employment an employee's promise that he would not become a union member.[2] Such legislation was categorized as unconstitutional intrusions on the liberty to contract. In the 1930's the Court abandoned the stringent dictates of "substantive due process." Since then legislatures and administrative agencies, if they choose, may place reasonable restrictions on the capacity of persons to enter into agreements on subjects which are of legitimate concern to society. For instance, the Uniform Commercial Code bars the enforcement of unconscionable contracts. Note that under the Code, a court, and not the parties, determines whether or not an agreement is unconscionable.[3] Similarly, courts may now find that parties enjoy rights and have obligations which are not called for by their agreement.

---

* University of Connecticut

MOTIVE

Assume that an apartment house landlord and a tenant enter into a month to month tenancy. Under the centuries-old approach to such an arrangement, either party is free to end the tenancy by simply providing the other with thirty days' notice of an intention to do so. If one enjoys a liberty to put an end to the tenancy, should his motive for deciding to do so be legally relevant? Until the 1960's why a landlord decided to terminate the tenancy was of no interest to the law. Then, in a landmark case, the court found that motive could be an appropriate consideration.

A month to month tenant, finding that his voiced objections to the conditions of the premises went unanswered by the landlord, notified the local housing authority of the apartment house's state of disrepair. Following an official inspection, the landlord was informed that he was legally obliged to correct more than forty violations of the housing law. Incensed by the consequences of the tenant's behavior, he gave the tenant thirty days' notice to quit the apartment. The tenant challenged the lawfulness of the termination of the tenancy. One of his arguments was that the landlord had been motivated by a desire to retaliate against him due to his having informed the authorities. Since the landlord's action was retaliatory, insisted the tenant, he was barred from bringing the tenancy to an end.

The tenant's position was rejected in the trial court as well as in the first appellate court. However, he was successful before the second appellate tribunal. It held that a landlord is barred from exercising the usual right to put an end to a month to month tenancy if the motive for the landlord's action is to retaliate against a tenant merely because he had exercised a legal right. Among the reasons the court gave for establishing what has come to be known as the retaliatory eviction doctrine is the fact that the failure to take motive into account would contribute to the deterioration of residential housing; that a tenant who leases an apartment is in effect purchasing a bundle of services in the same fashion that one buys consumer goods, and a tenant, like one who buys merchandise, is entitled to adequately enjoy the anticipated fruits of the purchase; and that it would be unrealistic to expect an apartment house tenant to expend his funds to correct outlawed housing conditions.[4]

Numerous courts have adopted the retaliatory eviction doctrine. A number of state legislatures have done likewise.

An employment contract may specify the period of time during which the employee, so long as he satisfies the terms of employment, may not be discharged. Collective bargaining agreements invariably prescribe the circumstances under which an employer may terminate one's employment. In general, however, employment arrangements are terminable at will. This means that at any time the employer, with or without reason, may discharge an employee. May an employer's motive for terminating an at-will employment entitle the discharged employee to damages?

In *Monge v. Beebe Rubber Company,*[5] the court found that there are instances when motive may render an employer liable for wrongful discharge.

The plaintiff, married, mother of four children, was discharged when she spurned her supervisor's advances. She did not have a contract specifying the length of her employment nor was she a beneficiary of a collective bargaining agreement. She sued for lost earnings. The employer insisted that she could be discharged at any time. The motive underlying her firing, it was insisted, was of no concern to the law. The court acknowledged that when employment is terminable at will an employee may be discharged without cause. Certainly, so far as business considerations are concerned, a court may not substitute its judgment for the employer's. Yet, an employer's power to terminate employment is not absolute. If discharge is motivated by other than a business-based factor, an employee is not necessarily without a remedy. There may be instances of a non-business motivated discharge which would allow the employee to recover damages. Here, the jury's verdict in favor of the plaintiff was consistent with the plaintiff's evidence that she was discharged because she had rejected her wooing superior. Termination due to such a non-business motive entitled her to recover damages on the grounds of wrongful discharge.

Motive has been held to be a relevant factor when a court passes on the right of an insurance company to exercise its right under a liability policy cancellation clause. Such a clause permits either party to cancel the agreement, without cause, upon giving the called-for notice. Following cancellation, the unearned portion of the premium is returned to the insured. The following case illustrates the relevance of motive.

An insurance company asked its insured, a practicing dentist, not to testify as an expert witness in a malpractice suit in which the defendant, a dentist, also was insured by the company. The request failed to convince the dentist not to testify. A judgment was entered against the dentist. The insurer, liable to pay the judgment, advised the dentist who had testified as an expert witness that his malpractice policy, which contained a right-to-cancel clause, was cancelled. Previously, the policy had been renewed time and time again. The court concluded that it would be against public policy to allow the company to exercise the contract's cancellation proviso. The policy had been terminated because the insured had testified against the insurer's interests. The court reasoned that if tribunals are to arrive at just results, litigants must be afforded the opportunity to use expert testimony. The insurer's action was intended to stymie the plaintiff in the prosecution of her malpractice case. To sustain the cancellation would be to support the insurer's retaliatory conduct. Similar future action would be encouraged, with the result that injured parties could be denied the opportunity to gather necessary evidence. By refusing to allow the company to cancel the policy, not only would the court bar the company from retaliating against the dentist who performed a civic obligation, but it might also deter other insurers from so behaving in the future.[6]

The number of areas of the law in which motive is a vital consideration in allocating rights and duties is already significant. Motive is certain to be an even more important measure of legally acceptable conduct in the future.

FAIRNESS

Fairness is a widely employed test of lawful behavior. Oftentimes the terms justice and fairness are used interchangeably. To be fair is to be just. When interpreting various portions of the Constitution of the United States courts frequently refer to the demands of fairness. If one were to trace the roots of statutes or agency regulations, or agency or court decisions, time and again he would find that the lawmakers' objectives were to assure fairness. In spite of the fact that a quest for fairness gives rise to a legal principle, it does not follow that the continuous application of the principle to related factual patterns will always yield a fair result. Fairness does not exist in a vacuum. What is or is not fair ultimately is determined by such distinctly unique factors as community aspirations; needs, whether they be real or imagined; and the discerned consensus of right and wrong. The community may be a hamlet, town, county, city, nation or even the earth. Except within narrow limits, there is no universal timeless test of what is fair and what is unfair.

The manner in which the Supreme Court has come to grips with defining the term due process is a striking example of judicial use of fairness as a test of lawfulness. Breathing life into the Fourteenth Amendment's guarantee that persons may not be deprived of life, liberty or property without due process of law, the Court has stated that due process guarantees persons fair procedures prior to the govenment's finally depriving them of life, liberty or property. Is there a precise once and for all time enumeration of what due process requires? No. The requisites of fundamental fairness are ever changing.

For example, in time of war the demands of due process are far less stringent than in time of peace. During World War II the Supreme Court sustained confining Japanese-Americans at relocation centers without affording them a trial on the question of whether or not there was in fact cause to deprive them of their liberty.[7] What could not help but rationally be regarded as unfair to the incarcerated individuals was on the judicial scale of concerns outweighed by the desire to fairly protect national security.

Numerous rules of contract law may be tested in terms of fairness. For instance, when should a mailed acceptance of an offer take effect? In the United States an acceptance generally is effective at the time of mailing. In some nations time of delivery to the offeror's place of business is determinative. There are jurisdictions in which a mailed acceptance creates a contract only when it in fact comes to the attention of the person charged with its negotiation. The proponents of each of these rules see their choice as guaranteeing fairness. The first mentioned rule is fair to the business which mailed the acceptance, since it has proceeded to communicate its intention by making use of a freely employed means of communication. The rule imposes contractual liability on the offeror from the moment the acceptance is mailed. Is this rule fair to the offeror should the letter of acceptance be delayed or lost? The time of delivery to the place of business test may be fair to the offeror and the offeree since once the letter is delivered to the offeror's place of business, suitable internal means should exist so as to promptly bring the acceptance to the attention of the appropriate executive. The requirement that actual knowledge of acceptance by the executive involved with the transaction is fair to the offeror since it does not impose a legal obligation until the responsible person in fact learns that the offer has been accepted. Which one of these rules passes muster under your sense of fairness? Why?

Businesses which sell merchandise on credit may at times lack the wherewithal to await payment on outstanding bills. In need of money, they transfer such indebtednesses for immediate cash. The indebtedness is known as an account receivable. The transfer is called an assignment. The business which transfers the account receivable is the assignor. The transferee is the assignee. In a legitimate assignment arrangement, an account receivable is assigned but once. The debtor, after all, is liable for no more than the sum agreed to be due.

On occasion, an assignor, perhaps responding to a dire immediate need for funds, assigns the same account receivable twice; maybe even three or more times. In such instances, which assignee is entitled to receive payment? Under what is commonly referred to as the American rule, except in a limited number of instances, the sum due belongs to the first assignee. Under the so-called English rule, which is followed by a minority of states, the first assignee who advises the debtor of an assignment is entitled to be paid. Which of these rules insures a fair result? Why?

Legislation directed at promoting fairness may designate specific forms of conduct as fair, or bar unfair behavior, without defining what is meant by the word unfair. When a statute states what specific types of conduct are required or outlawed, the legislature itself has decided the sorts of action which are fair or unfair. If a statute fails to state just what is meant by the term fair or unfair, the burden necessarily falls on an administrative agency or the judiciary to define fairness within the context of the statute.

The Fair Credit Reporting Act contains a series of directives as to the sort of information which may or may not be reported to one who wishes to be informed about a prospective employee or debtor. The Fair Credit Billing Act places a battery of obligations on creditors regarding the manner in which they must deal with debtors. The Bankruptcy Act classifies a debtor's transfer of assets prior to a bankruptcy proceeding as fraudulent when made or incurred for less than a fair consideration, if, as a result, the debtor is or will be rendered insolvent. The Labor Management Relations Act classifies a number of employers' practices as unfair labor practices and a series of union practices as unfair labor practices.

Curbing unfair methods of competition is one of the tasks Congress has assigned to the Federal Trade Commission. Speaking of this charge, the Supreme Court has observed that the Commission, when performing this function, is in substance acting as a court of equity, within the framework of the nation's antitrust laws.[8] By so categorizing the Commission's role the Court has mandated that the agency define fairness consistent with the demands of antitrust policy. Fairness, in this milieu, is synonymous with justice.

The Federal Communications Commission's fairness doctrine is an example of an administrative agency's use of the concept of fairness to arrive at a standard of required broadcast media behavior. This rule is based on the public's right to be informed. It requires broadcast media to offer balanced presentations on issues of public importance by providing for the dissemination of differing points of view. Radio and television operators must, when no sponsor is available, make free time available for the presentation of views opposed to already expressed positions.[9] Prior to the ban on cigarette broadcast advertising, the Commission required broadcasters to allocate time for the presentation of messages intended to persuade persons not to smoke. The next time you hear the broadcast of a non-sponsored reply to an already stated point of view on a matter of public interest remember: while the station may have provided the free time independent of the Commission's regulation, the time may have been provided because of the demands of the fairness doctrine.

The number of business transactions and ongoing business relationships in which the law expressly utilizes fairness as the determinative test of the rights and duties of the parties is infinite. The boundless applicability of fairness as the stated criterion of the demands of justice makes it impossible to arrive at a succinct statement of the legal system's overall test of fairness. In spite of the inherent ambiguity of fairness as a legal standard of right and wrong, fairness is certain to continue to be a frequently used test of the propriety of business conduct.

GOOD FAITH

Statutes may provide that good faith should be taken into account to determine which of the parties to a controversy should obtain a favorable judgment. The Uniform Commercial Code, for example, enumerates circumstances in which good faith must be taken into account to adjudge rights and duties. The Code defines good faith as "honesty in fact in the conduct or transaction concerned."[10]

One of the instances in which the Code expressly requires a person to act in good faith involves the exercise of an acceleration clause found in a promissory note. A promissory note is an agreement in which a party, the maker, promises to pay a sum of money to another, the payee. The note may be payable at a stated time. When it is, factors which may have an adverse impact on the maker's credit-worthiness do not alter the stated time of payment. A payee, in order to avoid holding a note beyond the time when it seems to be safe to call for payment, may demand that the note contain an acceleration clause. Such a clause may permit the payee, or one who later becomes the owner of the note, to demand payment before the due date if at any time he feels insecure. The Code provides that a demand for early payment made under such a clause must be made in good faith.[11] The effect of the code's limitation on the exercise of the power to speed up payment is to establish a requirement that one honestly feel insecure. The requirement bars abuse. However, should the maker be of the opinion that the power to accelerate was not exercised in good faith, the burden would fall on him to prove it.

Under the Model Business Corporation Act corporate powers are exercised by or under the authority of the board of directors. Similarly, corporate business and affairs are generally managed under the board's direction. Since most directorships are but part-time commitments, directors necessarily must make use of information, opinions, reports, and statements dealing with corporate matters which they receive from corporate officers and employees as well as professional persons such as lawyers and accountants. Under what circumstances, if any, should a director be free from liability for losses incurred by the corporation or by actual or potential stockholders, in the event reliance upon erroneous materials causes damage to the corporation or stockholders? The Model Act states that a director may rely on materials he received from corporate officers and employees as well as professional persons such as lawyers and accountants so long as he reasonably believes such persons merit confidence.[12] A director is not considered to be acting in good faith if he has (such) knowledge about a matter that would cause him to conclude that reliance on received information is unwarranted.[13] The good faith standard insulates honest directors from liability for damages traceable to information received from persons they can reasonably be expected to turn to for advice.

Aspects of the law of business crimes, like other segments of the criminal law, may take into account motive, fairness, and good faith. The recent case of *United States v. Fields* raises an unusual question of fairness in the criminal law. At this issue in *Fields* was the propriety of government officials proceeding against several executives allegedly guilty of business crimes. The executives had apparently violated federal law by manipulating stock prices. Their attorneys, fearful that the matter would be brought to the attention of the Security and Exchange Commission, advised the executives that to avoid criminal liability they should contact the Commission with a view toward arriving at a civil settlement. They accepted the advice. The attorneys arranged a meeting with Commission officials. At the very inception of the talks between counsel and officials, the latter were informed that the meeting had been arranged to arrive at a civil settlement so as to shield the executives from criminal liability. The officials remained silent. The attorneys supplied evidence which incriminated their clients. Negotiations were carried on for many months. During this time, the attorneys, on several occasions, insisted that the Commission's settlement demands were costly. They observed however, that a settlement was preferable to criminal prosecution. A party not involved in the purported wrongdoing, who was interested in replacing one of the executives as a director of the corporation whose stock had been manipulated, inquired of one of the Commission's officials if criminal prosecutions would follow. He was given a negative response. During the negotiations, a Commission official who had been fully aware of the executives' objective to avoid criminal liability informed the United States Attorney that once the civil matter had been resolved, the case would be referred for criminal prosecution. On the eve of the execution of the civil settlement consent decree, and after the Commission had advised the attorneys for the executives that they had a settlement, the Commission referred the matter to the United States Attorney for criminal presecution. Shortly thereafter but before an indictment had been secured on the very facts which the executives' attorneys had called to the attention of the Commission, the executives signed the settlement decree. It called for, among other things, the payment of over $500,000, their terminating their directorships, and withdrawal from the practice of law before the Commission of one of the executives who was also an attorney.

The court held that the executives could not be prosecuted for the criminal behavior which their attorneys reported to the Commission. The decision was based on a "totality of circumstances" test. In effect the court asked the question: If what had occurred between the attorneys and the Commission were to be viewed objectively, would it be reasonable for the defendants to conclude that a civil settlement would shield them from a criminal prosecution? The clients had been prodded by their attorneys to settle the matter, relying on counsel's having informed the Commission that they were proceeding so as to avoid criminal liability. Noting everything that had transpired between counsel and the Commission, and the Commission's attention, the court stated that in the circumstances of the case principles of equity and fairness required the Commission's representatives to promptly reveal to defense counsel that a criminal reference had been made. The Commission's non-disclosure of the *present fact* of a criminal reference, viewed in the context of all that had gone before, was held to be "inequitable and wrong."

American jurisprudence is certain to pay ever more attention to motive, fairness, and good faith in civil and criminal aspects of business law. The prevailing sense of right and wrong will continue to significantly influence the relevance as well as the constraints generated by considerations grouped under these labels.

overturned on appeal

ENDNOTES

1. Lochner v. New York, 25 S.Ct. 539 (1905).
2. Coppage v. Kansas, 236 U.S. 1 (1915).
3. §Z-302.
4. Edwards v. Habib, (D.C.Cir. 1968) 397 F.2d 687.
5. 316 A.2d 549 (N.H. 1974)
6. L'Orange v. Medical Protective Co., (6th Cir. 1968) 394 F.2d 57.
7. Korematsu v. United States, 323 U.S. 214 (1944).
8. F.T.C. v. Sperry and Hutchinson Co., 405 U.S. 233 (1972).
9. Columbia Broadcasting System v. Democratic National Committee, 412 U.S. 94 (1973).
10. §-201(19).
11. §1-208.
12. §25.
13. Id.
14. (D.C.S.D.N.Y. 1977) _____ F. Supp. _____

3

Some Jurisprudential Aspects of the Uniform Commercial Code

Bruce D. Fisher*

Everyone knows that oil and water do not mix. Similarly it may seem anomolous to mention the Uniform Commercial Code and jurisprudence in the same breath. "After all," some might say, "what relation does legal theory have to the mundane rules of commercial law?" It is true that U.C.C. rules are episodic at best since they resolve (and create) many factually unrelated disputes involving sales of goods, commercial paper, bank collections, investment securities, warehouse receipts and bills of lading, letters of credit, bulk sales, and security interests in personalty and fixtures.

The reason for discussing legal theory and commercial law in the same chapter lies in the strong jurisprudential undercurrent throughout the U.C.C. This is not to say that the U.C.C.'s drafters consciously tried to introduce jurisprudential theory into the code. Nonetheless they did, at least unconsciously, and an awareness of its presence helps to understand better a number of the U.C.C.'s provisions.

This chapter will first identify and discuss four recognized schools of jurisprudence. Second, several blackletter U.C.C. rules will be presented. Then the legal theory (or theories) supporting the rules will be discussed.

SOME JURISPRUDENTIAL THEORIES

Philosophers from at least the time of the Greeks have attempted to explain what the law is. From these attempts has arisen a branch of philosophy called jurisprudence. Jurisprudence deals with the meaning and objectives of law. Four major jurisprudential philosophies discussed here are positive law,

---

* The University of Tennessee

natural law, the historical school of jurisprudence, and the sociological school of law.

The term *positive law* suggests that positive law is the opposite of negative law. This, however, is not correct. The positive character of positive law comes from its being "laid down" or "posited" by someone on a given situation, not from its semantically positive expression, "Do something" (as opposed to "Don't do anything".). Thus a law that says "Don't do something" is every bit as much a positive law as is a law that says, "Do something." Who does the "positing" of law on a situation is of great importance to legal positivists. It must be the sovereign. Legal positivists usually do not quibble over the democratic, oligarchic, or monarchic character of the sovereign as long as sufficient power exists in the sovereign to enforce its rules. An Englishman named John Austin is credited with developing the positive law school of jurisprudence. Others who have followed his lead include Hans Kelsen and Oliver Wendell Homes, Jr.

Natural law is to be contrasted with positive law in the sense that natural law is what people think is right or fair. As such natural law might not coincide with positive law although it often will. Natural law is not law in the positivistic sense, but rather finds its source from either God or people's rational sense. In other words, natural law is not law as we commonly use the term law. Rather, it is what each person believes is right or fair independent of what the law orders us to do (or refrain from doing). Thus the positive law may well agree with what one thinks is right and fair or it may not. When there is disagreement tension exists. If the tension is severe and widespread enough, positive law will have to be changed. One of the problems of natural law stems from its source; since it comes from each person's view of what the law should be, it is very subjective. Each person could have a different view of what the law should be and hence it may be difficult, if not impossible, to reach a consensus on what course the positive law should take.

The *historic school* of jurisprudence was, at least in part, founded as a reaction to natural law thinkers who used natural law as the basis for overthrowing European monarchs, particularly in France. Historic jurisprudence was conceived by Savigny, a German nobleman. A valid law in Savigny's eyes was one which reflected deep-seated values of a nation. Savigny said that the long-standing customs of the people preclude sudden shifts in rules if the rules are to be valid. A society which valued private commerce would find it intolerable to be deprived of the right to enter contracts with other private persons. A society accustomed to purchasing alcoholic beverages would rebel if deprived of its spirits, as the adoption and repeal of the Prohibition Amendment proved. Savigny represented the "establishment" in his country. His historical philosophy conveniently justified the continuance of his prominent position and is useful to anyone defending an existing set of laws.

The *sociological school* is the final jurisprudential idea considered here. There are two branches of sociological jurisprudence. One was developed by the late Roscoe Pound, former dean of Harvard Law School. Pound believed law represented a balance struck between competing claims. Another major sociological jurisprudent, Eugene Ehrlich, regarded law as "norms of conduct." How people act determines what the positive law is. If people wish to enter into business partnerships, then the positive law should let them do it. If people wish to make contracts for the sale of goods, then the law should sanction such intercourse. A problem with the "norms approach" to defining law lies in the possible lowering of community standards in the name of accommodating people's desires. What people do and what they want to do is not necessarily what is best for them. Yet a norms approach would lead to this conclusion. An advantage of having norms of conduct define law lies in the fact that positive law will be obeyed.

Having seen several jurisprudential schools, it remains to present specific U.C.C. rules evidencing them.

POSITIVE LAW IN THE U.C.C.

Positive law is most obviously in evidence in the U.C.C. simply because the U.C.C. has been enacted into law by the legally constituted authority to pass such laws in each state—the legislature with the Governor's approval. To the extent that the courts have engaged in interstitial lawmaking to clarify ambiguities or fill gaps left by the U.C.C.'s drafters this, too, is positive law, since courts (judges) are empowered to make such law.

One of the more troubling questions dealt with in positive law concerns the possibility of a positive law's illegality. Put another way, can the sovereign enact an illegal law? Positive law theory answers "yes," because a number of legal theories are accepted as ways to overturn what would (if these theories were not invoked by a challenger) otherwise be regarded as positive law. For example, if a legislature and chief executive pass a law and it is successfully challenged and struck down as unconstitutional, then the "law" in question is no longer positive law. Legal theories other than unconstitutionality—void as contrary to public policy, for instance—exist to declare positive "laws" illegal. Although there has been some scholarly writing on the subject of the U.C.C.'s possible unconstitutionality, its constitutionality in general is not questioned today.

NATURAL LAW IN THE U.C.C.

Since every word of the U.C.C. is positive law, it is difficult to find a more pervasive jurisprudential influence in it. However, natural law has found its way into several U.C.C. sections. Perhaps the most prominent is section 2-302 which deals with unconscionable contracts. That section says:

(1) If the court as a matter of law finds the contract or any part of the contract to have been unconscionable at the time it was made the court may refuse to enforce the contract, or it may enforce the remainder of the contract without the unconscionable clause, or it may so limit the application of any unconscionable clause as to avoid any unconscionable result.

(2) When it is claimed or it appears to the court that the contract or any clause thereof may be unconscionable, the parties shall be afforded a reasonable opportunity to present evidence as to its commercial settings, purpose and effect to aid the court in making the determination.

The above language is all that section 2-302 says about unconscionability. It is generally thought that in defining a word, terms other than the word being defined should be used. Unfortunately the U.C.C. drafters did not observe this precept in defining unconscionability. Generally speaking, however, one would not be far from the mark if natural law's "right, just, and fair" definition were applied to define unconscionability. The drafters of section 2-302 were no doubt mindful of the uncertainty that the natural law doctrine could introduce into commercial settings if impressionable jurors were given the final word on whether a contract were unconscionable. Therefore they drafted the section so that it circumscribes unconscionability considerably by leaving the meaning of unconscionability to the judge—not the jury. Of course judges are as susceptible to bias as are juries, all of which illustrates another facet of natural law: its subjectivity.

There are other examples of natural law in the Uniform Commercial Code. In section 1-201(19) the words "good faith" are defined to mean honesty in fact. Section 1-102(3) declares ". . . that the obligations of good faith, diligence, reasonableness and care prescribed by this Act may not be disclaimed by agreement . . ." What could be more representative of the fairness, rightness, and justice that is the essence of natural law? Carried to the ultimate extreme, one could say that natural law also permeates the U.C.C. because obviously its drafters would not have installed rules they believed to be wrong or unfair.

HISTORIC JURISPRUDENCE IN THE U.C.C.

Many longstanding commercial law rules antedating the U.C.C. are incorporated in it. The basic rule that private parties may make a contract is recognized in Article 2 of the U.C.C., which applies to transactions in goods. The idea that individuals can alter their situation by making private agreements was recognized long ago by the legal historian, Sir Henry Maine. His now famous utterance, "the movement of the progressive societies has hitherto been a movement from status to contract," meant that a civilization advances when people cease having their destinies determined by their social status at birth (nobleman versus serf; today, man versus woman) and instead control their own future. People control their growth and development by the voluntary agreements (contracts) they enter. Article 2 of the U.C.C., by recognizing the contract in sale of goods situations, carries forward a longstanding notion and thereby exemplifies the historic school of jurisprudence. Other commercial law ideas long recognized prior to the U.C.C., such as negotiable instruments and creditor security claims on personal property and fixtures are now, as before, recognized, albeit under different nomenclature ("security interests" rather than "liens," "conditional sales," and the like).

U.C.C. continuance of both negotiable instruments and creditor security claims suggests a basic historic school viewpoint: that although legal changes can occur (as the U.C.C. has changed prior law) they must be modest, incremental modifications if they are to be readily obeyed and adjusted to by the community.

At one point, in section 1-103, the U.C.C. expressly carries forward general legal and equitable principles to the extent needed to supplement U.C.C. rules. The exact language is as follows:

> Unless displaced by the particular provisions of this Act, the principles of law and equity, including the law merchant and the law relative to capacity to contract, principal and agent, estoppel, fraud, misrepresentation, duress, coercion, mistake, bankruptcy, or other validation or invalidating cause shall supplement its provisions.

Legal tradition marches on hand in hand with change, or as the French are fond of saying, "The more things change, the more things stay the same."

SOCIOLOGICAL JURISPRUDENCE IN THE U.C.C.

Pound's balancing approach to defining law is captured in section 2-403(2) of the U.C.C. which provides:

> Any entrusting of possession of goods to a merchant who deals in goods of that kind gives him (or her) the power to transfer all rights of the entruster to a buyer in the ordinary course of business.

The section hypothesizes two innocent persons, one of whom must lose because a merchant either negligently or intentionally disposes of a customer's goods, left in the merchant's custody, to another customer, a good faith purchaser for value without notice of the prior customer/entruster's rights to the goods. The U.C.C. strikes a balance in this section in favor of the buyer in the ordinary course of business, by reducing customers' apprehensions that goods they purchase in a store may later be legally taken from them by another person.

Ehrlich's "norms of conduct" sociological definition of law ("How people act determines what the law is") finds support in several U.C.C. sections. Section 1-102(2) (b) notes that the underlying U.C.C. policies and purposes are

> to permit the continued expansion of commercial practices through custom, usage and agreement of the parties.

When the "custom" and "usage" terms are used, Ehrlich's ideas are in evidence. The U.C.C., like Ehrlich, is willing to let private parties' conduct shape the law, within limits. This makes a great deal of sense in an economy founded on notions of private initiative and innovation.

A concrete example of conduct's shaping the law occurs in section 2-207(2), covering added terms in acceptance of a contract offer for the sale of goods.

The common law rule has been—and continues to be for realty and services—that an acceptance must conform exactly with the terms of an offer. The reason is to protect the offeror from being thrust into an unanticipated bargain by an overly zealous acceptor who adds terms in the acceptance. The mode of conducting business has changed from individually negotiated, personalized contracts of yesteryear to form contracts designed to satisfy the high velocity of business today. Hence business offerors make their offers on preprinted forms and acceptors make their acceptances on preprinted confirmation forms. Both offer and confirmation (acceptance) forms contain boilerplate language designed to protect the sender of each document. The language of such forms seldom "dovetails" to satisfy strict common law standards for acceptance. Yet businesspeople need to have some document to refer to as a contract in the event performance fails. Enter UCC 2-207 which says that an express acceptance with added terms is effective. This section then provides a set of criteria to determine whether the additional or different terms are a part of the contract. Businesspeople assume that some combination of the documents used in the contract formation stage will control their agreement and 2-207 gives validity to this assumption. The prior law did not. This is an excellent example of the tailoring of positive law to the workings of modern business conduct.

CONCLUSION

The Uniform Commercial Code is of comparatively recent vintage as legal developments go, having been enacted first by Pennsylvania in the early fifties and by all states (at least in part) in the period up to the present. As the above discussion illustrates, the U.C.C. contains elements of several schools of legal thought. This chapter by no means has attempted an exhaustive treatment of the jurisprudence of the U.C.C. There are many other schools of legal thought, examples of which could be found in the U.C.C. The utility of studying legal philosophy in conjunction with the U.C.C. lies in the tests jurisprudence provides to judge the validity of the code as well as the improved understanding it provides of the U.C.C.

As positive law, the U.C.C. satisfies many of the criteria which the natural, positive, historic, and sociological schools establish for legal validity. This helps explain the U.C.C.'s widespread adoption even though it departs in some respects from prior commercial law doctrine.

Part II

Social Responsibility

There is a great deal of concern today over business ethics and the social responsibility of large business. Many unethical practices have been described in the media, and business is criticized by many groups for taking a too narrow view of its basic responsibilities.

Business schools are beginning to respond to this concern and criticism by including coverage of ethical issues at various points within the curriculum. A natural place for such coverage is in introductory law courses. Law and morality often intertwine. The questioning method typically used in the teaching of collegiate law courses lends itself nicely to the introduction of ethical questions. Further, law often represents a potential remedy for unethical acts. Finally, a comprehensive discussion of corporate social responsibility cannot ignore proposed changes in the corporate law.

In Chapter 4 Professor Dunfee introduces the topic of ethics. The basic philosophical theories of ethics are presented followed by a discussion of values especially pertinent to our business system. The chapter closes with a series of case problems involving the application of ethical principles and values to actual business situations.

The next chapter by Professor Wolfe deals with the general question of social responsibility by focusing on two important current cases, *Reserve Mining* and *Ford Motor* (the Pinto case). In presenting these two cases studies Professor Wolfe deals with the vitally important question of to what extent corporations are driven to engage in questionable practices by the great emphasis on business profitability in modern society.

Professor Shaw closes this Part with an analysis of the competing, often mutually exclusive policies that must be considered in the area of corporate social responsibility. His specific emphasis is on environmental law. The

Clean Air Act is analyzed and then a brief situation study is presented concerning the question of limited liability of utilities for nuclear accidents.

The three chapters in this Part progress from the theoretical to the specific. All of the chapters present problems demonstrating the perplexing nature of the policy issues in this field. There are no simple answers. The reader, however, should come away with an appreciation of the kinds of issues that arise and of the basic alternative remedies available to deal with them.

4

Business Ethics

Thomas W. Dunfee*

How would you respond if someone asked "Are you an ethical person?" Like most people, you would probably answer "Yes, I think that basically I am an ethical person."

But suppose that your questioner responds with a more difficult proposition: "How do you justify your conclusion that you are ethical?" If you are typical, you will probably have some trouble answering this one; and answers given by a group of people will probably vary widely. Justifications likely to be offered might include the following:

I'm ethical because

- I avoid hurting others
- I sometimes help others
- I never knowingly break the law
- I am religious
- Other people think that I am ethical
- I follow personal standards that are themselves ethical
- I am a good American
- Deep down inside I know that I'm ethical

The two questions asked in the first paragraphs are not merely academic. You will face situations throughout your personal and professional life in which you will be required to make ethical choices. Sometimes the issue will be clearly presented—someone may want you to assist him in cheating on his taxes by paying him in cash instead of by check, or you may be asked bluntly to pay a commercial bribe. Probably, however, the issue will be more subtle. Instead of simply asking for a bribe, a purchasing agent may propose a complex deal that results in his receiving a special fee for a "service" to be rendered. You know, however (if you wish to think about it), that the fee is grossly dis-

*The Wharton School, University of Pennsylvania

proportionate to the value of the service to be rendered—if there is any service at all.

What will *you* do in such cases? Some people avoid characterizing these issues in ethical terms. Instead, they think solely in terms of whether an action is legal. And a few (one would hope just a very few) may even think solely in terms of whether they are likely to get caught. However, most people would try to consider the ethical consequences of their behavior in such circumstances. The rest of this chapter will present some background for such considerations by 1) summarizing the basic philosophical theories of ethics, 2) identifying special ethical values relevant to the business world, and 3) presenting several problems that may serve as a vehicle for class discussion of applied business ethics.

PHILOSOPHICAL ETHICAL THEORY

There is no single, generally accepted theory of values in the field of philosophy that can be used to answer questions involving business ethics. Instead, various theories of ethics and values have been proposed and developed and each, at any given point in time, has had its own proponents. Before identifying the major ethical theories a few preliminary comments are in order.

In answer to the question "Why are you ethical?" it was suggested that some people might say that they were regarded as ethical by their friends or that they were good Americans. Such answers are based on an assumption that ethics are entirely relative to culture. A relativistic approach to ethics would require us to conclude that slavery was moral in the United States in 1800. No true standards of evaluation are involved in a relativistic approach to ethical values. For this reason, most philosophers today reject the approach of establishing ethical standards through the use of public opinion polls.

Another suggested answer was that one is moral because one avoids breaking the law. This view has several problems associated with it. One is that it implies that no law can be immoral. Again, slavery would have been moral up to the time of the Emancipation Proclamation. A second problem is that this view assumes that the law and the rules of ethical behavior are and should be co-extensive. In fact, the law does not equate with many precepts of ethical behavior. Many promises can be broken (for example, a promise to make a gift) and one may often lie without incurring legal consequences. Further, many authorities are of the opinion that the law should not attempt to enforce standards of moral behavior. They argue that such a goal is not a proper objective for a modern legal system. This conclusion is based on the assumption that certain aspects of morality cannot be legislated. Further, the choice of which moral standards to enact into law involves enormous difficulties.

Some people just "feel" that they are ethical. If such feelings are accepted as evidence of morality, then ethics is reduced to a matter of personal taste. Again, if an individual honestly felt that slavery was moral, then to that individual it would be. Such a subjective test would run counter to a theory of ethical values. Most philosophers reject such a view and instead hold to some variation of the following theories.

UTILITARIANISM

Under this theory actions are right or ethical to the extent that they promote happiness. Happiness is judged on a net basis in relation to all of society. The focus is on the result of a proposed action rather than the character of the action itself. For example, a drug company may wish to market a drug that relieves toothache. The drug is better than any other for this purpose, but it also causes nausea in some people. A utilitarian would conclude that the reduction of pain in society more than cancels out the slight increase in nausea and is ethical.

There are two forms of utilitarianism, *act*-utilitarianism and *rule*-utilitarianism. Act utilitarianism involves evaluation of actions on an ad hoc case-by-base basis. A particular type of action may thus be ethical in one situation because it produces a net promotion of happiness and unethical in another situation because it produces a net lessening of happiness.

Rule-utilitarianism uses the basic net happiness test to establish rules that are then applied generally. Thus, if a certain type of action is unethical by virtue of such a rule, then it is always unethical regardless of an individual effect of increasing happiness. For instance, a rule-utilitarian might conclude that because commercial bribes are generally secretive, illegal and inefficient, they should not be paid. The rule-utilitarian would then refuse to pay a single bribe even though that particular payment might produce desirable economic and social consequences such as the creation of new jobs and higher profits.

KANTIANISM

A major philosopher, Immanuel Kant (1724-1804), believed that the principle upon which an act is based is more important than the consequences of the act. A moral act is one produced by a sense of duty founded on a rational moral principle. Such action is moral even though it does not produce a net increase in societal happiness. Conversely, an unethical act is one based on naked inclination unsupported by a sense of duty.

What is an example of a rational moral principle? Kant provides one in his well known "categorical imperative." A person should only engage in acts that he would be willing to see become universal standards. This principle treats everyone as a moral equal. One is to avoid actions that would create problems if everyone did them. For example, if each retail business selling the same branded product decided to take a "free ride" on the advertising of its competitors regarding that product, there would be no advertising left to take a free ride on.

Further, under the Kantian theory, one is to avoid actions which, if accepted as a general standard, would defeat one's own legitimate interests. If an insurance agent refuses to insure anyone over fifty, the agent himself will not be able to obtain insurance at fifty if this conduct becomes universal. Thus, Kant emphasizes general moral principles.

NATURAL LAW

Natural law as a source of standards of ethical conduct is seen as principles emanating from a divine being or some other ultimate source. There is thus a "natural good" which is discoverable by man. Man's obligation is to use reason and intelligence to discover that good.

Although natural law as a concept stands independently of a particular religion, some theologians/philosophers have tied natural law theories into the precepts of a particular religion. Thus, if a religion views fornication as immoral, then obtaining business by the use of sexual favors is unethical. Similarly, selling birth control devices to certain individuals might be considered immoral. In this way, deductive reasoning is used to apply natural law ethical standards to specific situations.

SOCIAL JUSTICE

A modern philosopher, John Rawls, has proposed a theory of social justice as a basis for ethical standards. Under this view society as a whole "contracts" to establish standards of ethics (justice) that would govern social interaction. The authority of the standards emanates from society's willing acceptance of them. The "contract" is implied rather than express.

This concept is democratically based with majority interests limited by certain minority rights. The overriding limitation would be a concept of "fairness." Each person would have certain fundamental liberties; beyond these, inequalities would be allowed if they furthered the societal good. Thus, the Kantian and utilitarian approaches are merged in Rawl's theory.

BUSINESS VALUES

What specific values must be considered in evaluating problems involving business ethics? There are many that could be suggested. In a chapter of this length it is impossible to do more than provide a few examples.

As these examples of business values are presented the reader should keep in mind that none of them should be considered preeminent. In the context of a particular ethical decision consideration of different values may lead toward mutually exclusive conclusions. Some comparative evaluation of all relevant values is necessary in resolving any problem of business ethics.

The description of business values which follows represents an amalgamation of generally accepted values and the author's personal values. Not everyone would agree that each of these categories represents a significant business ethic. No inference regarding the relative merit of the values in intended.

ECONOMIC EFFICIENCY

Specific business values are intimately related to the role of business in our society. The primary goal of business is to produce and distribute effectively quality goods and services which satisfy legitimate consumer desires. In making specific decisions managers must be concerned with whether or not they are efficiently serving society.

PROFIT

The reward and incentive to business for performing its economic function is profit. Investors and creditors put money into a company because they expect profits; and managers of a business enterprise have a legal obligation to operate the company in a manner consistent with legitimate owner and creditor expectations. Some have argued that this is the *sole* obligation of business managers. However, most fair-minded people disagree and argue that business managers must recognize a broader range of values.

HUMANISM

Humanism is concerned with human life and well-being. Many products can maim or kill if carelessly made or defectively designed. Regardless of our role in society we all have an obligation to refrain from knowingly harming others and to act with care. Every legal person, corporate and human, must act in a civilized concerned manner toward others.

RESPECT

Everyone should be treated with respect. An employer may have such control over an employee that the employer has the *power* to treat the employee with disrespect. For example, an employer may subject an employee to unwanted sexual advances.

Respect may also be a factor in negotiations with other businesspeople. A party in a strong bargaining position may be able to "serve a slice of humble pie" to a weaker party. Having the power to act in such a manner does not make it right. The business value of respect should be considered.

OBLIGATION

The legal system recognizes and enforces a wide range of obligations. At the same time there are situations in which industry trade practice or a prior course of dealing between the parties recognizes an obligation that courts would not enforce. A few states, for example, deny the enforceability of requirements contracts whereby a buyer promises to buy all of his or her requirements of a designated commodity from a particular seller. Even though the state law will not enforce such agreements on the technical ground of insufficiency of consideration, many such contracts are entered into. In complying with the terms of these agreements the parties give recognition to a form of obligation other than that based on the law of contract.

HONESTY

Trust is essential to an efficient marketplace. Businesspeople must be able to rely upon the representations and disclosures of others. Honesty is the foundation of trust. If merchants anticipate dishonesty, then time and money will be spent on checking the validity of specific representations. Although some checking is prudent, if merchants have to incur significant checking costs because of widespread dishonesty the economic system becomes less efficient.

Honesty involves acting in good faith and also requires that all representations convey accurate information. Half-truths which will foreseeably mislead are not honest. The test is—how will the hearer/reader interpret the statement?

Most misrepresentations involve statements of fact. I misrepresent to you that my car has been driven 40,000 miles when, in fact, is has been driven 60,000. A misrepresentation can also occur in regard to a statement of value. If I tell you that my car is in "good" condition when, in fact, that is not my opinion, I have been dishonest.

A more difficult problem is determining when it is dishonest to remain silent. In most circumstances the failure to volunteer information would not be dishonest. However, if one party knows 1) that the other party has made a reasonable misassumption, or 2) that there is an undisclosed fact that is materially relevant to the relationship between the parties, then honesty requires disclosure.

The law of fraud deals with many of the issues discussed in this section. However, this law does not precisely encompass the boundaries of the business value of honesty. An innocent misrepresentation may not be dishonest, but it may entitle the victim of the misrepresentation to legal relief. On the other hand, a half-truth or a misrepresentation of one's opinion of value may dishonest but may not be subject to legal remedy.

LOYALTY

Loyalty is a highly important business value. Firms in a supplier-buyer relationship may do business over a number of years. During that time each party may have given special "breaks" to the other. The supplier may have extended credit beyond the usual term when the buyer had special problems. The buyer may have allowed the seller to meet or nearly meet the lower price of a competitor in order to keep the account. As a result of such actions the parties will have built up a sense of loyalty toward each other.

Loyalty is usually a mutual relationship in that two parties feel loyal to the other. Loyalty may exist between employers and employees, professionals and their client businesses, or any two business entities that have a direct commercial relationship. Someone that has had a long and satisfactory relationship with a particular firm will not incautiously switch and start dealing with another firm. Thus, loyalty helps bring about stability in our economic system.

CASE PROBLEMS

The following cases are presented for class discussion. They are designed to demonstrate the application of ethical principles to particular business situations. Identify the competing business values that are involved in the factual problems and then try to work toward a resolution of the problem by evaluating the merits of the competing values. It is suggested that a small group of students be assigned to present a proposed solution to each problem. Then the class as a whole would discuss the suggested solution.

1. Goodhealth Drug Company
   You have just been elected to a three year term as a director of the Goodhealth Drug Company. You have no other affiliation with the company. You

are expected to attend six meetings a year. As yet you have not been elected to any committees on the board. You will receive $6000 per year, plus expenses, plus $300 a meeting. One week prior to your first board meeting you receive a report concerning the company's drug Colstop. The highlights of the report are as follows:

- Colstop was introduced 14 months ago. The drug controls cholesterol.
- Colstop accounted for 15% of last month's sales and has been the primary contributor to a dramatic upturn in sales and earnings.
- Goodhealth is planning a major secondary offer of stock in three months which will have a major impact on the growth of the company.
- You have preliminary evidence from the field that the drug successfully controls cholesterol in 50% of the cases in which it is used.
- There is no comparable drug on the market.
- During the past four months your company has received reports of 18 cases in which severe cataracts have developed after prolonged use of Colstop. One involved a nine year old boy.
- The drug has been taken by over 400,000 people.
- The company reported the 18 cases to the FDA and they have announced that they will be investigating the drug.
- Doctors know of the reported instances of cataracts and they still prescribe the drug.
- Senior managment has just discovered that a zealous middle level employee doctored research reports that were sent to the FDA. The original report stated that "slightly less than 5% of the test mice developed cataracts after prolonged use." That sentence was removed from the summary report and the primary data were changed also so that no mice were listed as having developed cataracts.
- Goodhealth's research director states that the actual results regarding the mice don't show a cause/effect relationship between the drug and the cataracts.

What would you do in this situation? Explain your proposed actions by reference to the material presented in this chapter.

2. The Lab Technician

You are employed as a research technician by Goodhealth Drug Company. You ran a series of tests of Colstop on mice. You wrote in your report that many mice developed cataracts and lost hair when injected with the drug. You later saw the copy of the report that went to the top level management of Goodhealth and which also went to the F.D.A. Several of your sentences had been deleted and nothing was mentioned about cataracts. You report this to your superior. Your superior becomes angry and tells you to go back and change reports so that there is no reference to the cataracts.

You earn $21,000 a year at your job, you are widowed and are the sole support of three young children. Jobs of this caliber are hard to find. What do you do? Why? What ethical principles are involved?

3. You are employed as a work-study student by Ivy University. You go into a camera shop in the university area and buy a $300 camera for your own use.

The salesman asks if you work for the University and you say "yes." He then suggests that you put down that you are buying the camera for a university department because that would save $18 sales tax.

You hesitate. He says, "Everyone else does it. Anyway the state doesn't need the money." He writes up the slip naming a University department as buyer and doesn't charge you tax. What do you do? Why?

4. You are an engineering consultant to mining firms. Surestrike Mining hires you to do two jobs for $5,000 each. One is to evaluate a particular potential mine. You are familiar with the site and are sure that your report would be negative. What do you tell them?

The second job is to evaluate a producing mine. You do so and discover that the mine has moved under adjacent property owned by West Virginia Mining and that Surestrike does not have mineral rights to the coal being mined.

You report to Surestrike that they are infringing on the mineral rights of West Virginia Mining. They thank you and pay you. Six months later you discover Surestrike is still mining under that property and that they have not notified West Virginia Mining of your findings. Your contract with Surestrike provided that you would not disclose any findings to a third party. What do you do? What ethical considerations are involved?

5

The Modern Corporation and The Failure of Social Theory

Arthur D. Wolfe*

For the past 20 years Reserve Mining Co. has been dumping thousands of tons of residue *per day* into Lake Superior. It was first believed that their discharge of "harmless sand" would not damage the environment. However, 10 years ago it was reported that the *daily* discharge from Reserve of 67,000 tons of taconite waste contained substantial quantities of asbestos-like fibers which have found their way into the drinking water of the residents of Duluth. As early as 1969, Reserve Mining Co. was informed by the federal government that the discharge poses a substantial health threat to the humans living around the lake. Reserve has responded by fighting every court opinion, every order and every fine and the company has been successful to the extent that today the discharge continues and will continue until at least 1980. In recent years Reserve Mining Co. has earned a 90% *yearly* return on the invested capital. Reserve's own records reveal they could afford on-land disposal without damaging their competitive position but have postponed such disposal as long as possible.

The unofficial reports of a recent trial against Ford Motor Co. reveal that when Ford engineers designed the Pinto they were aware of the extremely dangerous placement and construction of the fuel tank. It appears that management consciously weighed the cost of anticipated litigation against the savings realized by the cheap construction and opted for the more dangerous alternative. Ford is a very successful corporation; Ford's fourth quarter 1977 profits are estimated at between $380 and $395 million.

How is this undesirable corporate behavior to be explained? This chapter is a search for a rational explanation of and a remedy for such behavior. The thesis will be advanced that our ideas about what is socially, economically and legally desirable are founded upon tradition; and that these tradition-bound ideas have failed to account for the impact on our society of the modern corporation, and particularly, the impact caused by the structure of the modern

*Michigan State University

corporation. This failure presents us with a paradox; we must assume that the managements of Reserve Mining and Ford believe they are acting in a socially desirable manner when they seek to maximize their profit—profit-maximizing acts are consistent with our whole prevailing social ideology which predicts that the general welfare of our society is served by such activity. Yet, it is the pursuit of profit by large corporations that, more than any other single source, threatens both our environment and our bodily safety.

A resolution of the paradox, it will be argued, does not involve the standard of profit. Instead, the resolution lies in directing our attention to the structure of the modern corporation. This structure, which facilitates profit maximization, minimizes the perception of the hard-to-measure costs of our society of the production of a good. We must increase the perception or awareness by corporate management of the full impact of their decisions.

The examination of this thesis will be presented in three parts. The first part examines the nature of our current ideology defining socially desirable commercial behavior. The second part presents in detail some of the facts involved in the litigation against Reserve Mining Co. and Ford. The final part makes some suggestions for confronting the threats to our present society posed by the modern corporation.

ON THE SIGNIFICANCE OF CONVENTIONAL WISDOM

The first requirement of an understanding of contemporary economic and social life is a clear view of the relation between events and the ideas which interpret them.
J.K. Galbraith, *The Affluent Society* 3rd ed., p. 6 (1976).

In the 1950's, noted Harvard economist, John Kenneth Galbraith, suggested the term "conventional wisdom" as a key to understanding current social and economic phenomena.[1] Conventional wisdom associates truth with that which is acceptable and familiar. Our American notions about what is socially, economically or legally desirable are organized around and based upon what the community *as a whole* finds acceptable or convenient. We approve of and promote that which we best understand. Over time the competition between the old policies and the new is usually resolved in favor of the former because the strategic advantage lies with that which has always existed. The accepted ideas become increasingly elaborate as the entire business-government-education complex devotes more and more resources to justifying established, accepted, self-serving ideas and practices. The conventional wisdom develops a literature, even a mystique, and ultimately becomes more or less synonymous with sound scholarship; thus, its position becomes virtually impregnable.[2]

Conventional wisdom dictates that the best method for the distribution of most industrial goods in the American economy is to allow purchasers and sellers to bargain freely in an established market for the goods. If there are many sellers and purchasers in the market, the price of the good sold will tend toward the cost of the last good provided to the market, and unreasonable or monopolistic profits will be eliminated. Movement of resources between markets is assured by assuming that where some markets are more profitable than others, they will attract resources. This results in more sellers and ultimately a lower priced good. When a market becomes unprofitable, resources will leave. This flow of resources to and from industrial markets resulting in lower prices of the goods produced is caused by each individual pursuing his or her own selfish desire to maximize return on investment. No central authority is needed to guarantee the maximization of society's welfare. It is done by an "invisible hand" guided only by individual greed. One must admit there is a ring of "truth" to this widely accepted and simplistically beautiful model of how our economy should be organized.

The conventional wisdom recognizes several corollaries to this general theory. The role of government is not to interfere with the industrial markets because this "distorts" the markets and inevitably results in inefficiencies. However, the government does have a role to play. It is to ensure, through its laws, that the "invisible hand" first recognized by Adam Smith continues to move freely. Thus, even most conservatives believe the government legitimately passes and enforces laws protecting the competitiveness of markets.

The more fundamental corollary equates the maximization of total welfare with profit. Conventional wisdom acknowledges that the participants in every industrial market have a duty to act in a socially responsible way. This duty is perceived by most participants, and is discharged by acting in a way which maximizes profit. When the duty to make a profit conflicts with a proposed course of action which would serve some other objective, the conventional wisdom dictates that the participant must choose the profit maximizing opportunity. This is especially true when a *corporation* is making the decisions, because corporate management has a duty to the owners of the enterprise to earn a return on their investment. As Nobel Laureate economist Milton Friedman has observed, when corporate management sacrifices an opportunity to earn a profit in order to achieve some other socially desirable objective (such as hiring and training the hard-core unemployed) they are not only infringing on the domain of the political process but they are betraying shareholders.[3]

Conventional wisdom accommodates itself not to an ever changing reality, but to the believer's desired view of the world. So, the conventional wisdom is not threatened by new ideas—they can be rationalized and reconciled in terms of the believer's values and perceptions of reality. The real threat to the conventional wisdom is the march of events.[4]

CONVENTIONAL WISDOM AND THE RISE OF THE MODERN CORPORATION

The corporation has, in fact, become both a method of property tenure and a means of organizing economic life. Grown to tremendous proportions, there may be said to have evolved a "corporate system"—as there was once a feudal system—which has attracted to itself a combination of attributes and powers, and has attained a degree of prominence entitling it to be dealt with as a major social institution.

A. Berle and G. Means, *The Modern Corporation and Private Property*, 1 (1932).

The conventional, simplistic model of how our economy operates or should operate to distribute industrial goods has failed to account for the rise of the modern corporate enterprise. The older conventional wisdom was based upon the writings of Adam Smith. Adam Smith's philosophy and economics were based upon the observation that humans are at once selfish (individualistic) and social beings. They desire to, on the one hand, maximize their own wealth and, on the other, seek approbation. He reconciled these two competing notions by asserting that the reason humans work is to gain the favor of others. He said:

> For to what purpose is all the toil and bustle of this world? What is the end of avarice and ambition, of the pursuit of wealth, of power, and pre-eminence? . . . what are the advantages we propose by that great purpose of human life which we call bettering our condition? *To be observed, to be attended to, to be taken notice of with sympathy, . . . and approbation, are all the advantages which we can propose to derive from it.* [5] *(emphasis added)*

Since commercial activity was brought about by individuals who were desiring to be well thought of in a public sense, the individuals would self regulate their commercial activity so as not to inflict damage on others or invoke the public wrath. Smith again states:

> In the race for wealth, and honours . . . (he) may run as hard as he can and strain every nerve and every muscle, in order to outstrip all his competitors. But if he should jostle, or throw down any of them, the indulgence of the spectators is entirely at an end. It is a violation of fair play, which they cannot admit of. [6]

Sellers in the markets of the 18th and early 19th centuries were mostly single individuals who most probably produced the product and marketed it. Then it was appropriate to build a theory on the assumptions that a seller (as a human) had: 1) complete information about the entire production and distribution process and market conditions, and 2) owned the assets of production or, at least, had some property at risk in the venture. *Such a seller would be particularly sensitive to the quantitative and qualitative demands of the "spectators" associated with the market.* In many instances such a seller would adjust both the products produced and general commercial conduct in response to those viewing or trading in the market for the product. The response could be predicted because the seller could be identified by those in the market and held *personally accountable* for the undesirable commercial activity.

While the traders in most industrial markets today differ radically from those of the 19th century, the prevailing social theory is still based upon the conventional wisdom which assumes all traders are human beings rather than corporations. For example, when the noted economist, Paul Samuelson, is introducing the general ideal of perfect competition in his best selling textbook, he states:

Perfect competition exists *only* in the case where no *farmer, businessman* or *laborer* is a big enough part of the total market to have any personal influence on market price;[7] (emphasis added)

By defining the ideal model of perfect competition in terms of a human actor ("farmer," "businessman," "laborer"), Samuelson is contributing to the perpetuation of the myth that significant traders are human (indeed today, there are human traders, but they are not significant in terms of the total value of manufactured goods).

The conventional assumption about the character of sellers in most industrial markets in this country is inaccurate, and it may result in a condition which seriously threatens our welfare. American corporate enterprise accounts for most of the total value of manufactured goods produced and sold in this country. The structure of large corporations (especially the largest 200 corporations) differs drastically from the so-called rational decision maker in the conventional model. Most large corporations are broken into many divisions and subsidiaries which separate the designer from the producer, the producer from the distributor, and the distributor from the seller; and they are directed by a team of managers who control the enterprise but do not own it. *The decision makers are effectively insulated from both the market and the shareholder-owners.* In this relative isolation, the decision makers still behave as Adam Smith suggested: they attempt to maximize profit. But, and this is where the failure of our social theory is apparent, the conventional view assumed the event producing the profit was to be evaluated together with other alternatives which would satisfy the "spectators." A decision depended upon a perception of how others in the market or associated with it would view those responsible for producing the product. As the human decision makers of the 20th century have withdrawn from direct contact with the production process and the market, they have had to rely more on the objective standard of profit to judge performance. The more subtle, human, subjective responses by those in the market cannot be measured and have thus been minimized in corporate decision making.

I am not ignoring the fact that major corporate decisions are based upon a "cost-benefit" analysis approach. The point is that in today's corporate board rooms, the perception of what is a cost and what is a benefit is not an accurate one. In numerous situations, intuitive, humane judgments which were possible under the commercial circumstances of the 19th century are replaced by a framework for decision making which overemphasizes profit. Profit is overemphasized because the decision makers are so removed from the production process and the market that they cannot judge the product's impact in any other terms than conventionally recognized costs. Thus, well-meaning, sensitive people overemphasize profit because the results of the decision cannot be perceived by them. The consequences of this overemphasis are apparent every time one picks up a newspaper, book or scholarly journal on commercial behavior. Consider the following case studies.

RESERVE MINING COMPANY

This company will be a responsible company and we will recognize our legal liabilities.

(Comment by H.S. Taylor, Mines Engineer, Reserve Mining Company, quoted in *United States v. Reserve Mining Co.* 412 F. Supp. 709, 1976)

In 1956 Reserve Mining Company (Reserve) began large-scale iron ore processing on the shore of Lake Superior. Reserve was and is a corporation owned jointly by two large steel companies, Armco Steel Corporation (Armco) and Republic Steel Corporation (Republic). Reserve was purchased to make the production of steel less costly to its giant owners. Instead of extracting and shipping all of the unrefined iron ore from the rich deposits in Minnesota to the owners' plants in the midwest, the iron ore would be separated from waste matter in Minnesota and then shipped in the form of iron ore pellets to the steel plants. A major consideration of the owners in locating the plant at Silver Bay, Minnesota, was the proximity not only to the deposits but also to the "great trough" in Lake Supeior into which Reserve would discharge its effluent, "harmless sand."[8] On-land disposal of the waste (tailings) was apparently considered and rejected in favor of disposal into the lake because it was less costly.[9] The effluent would pose no substantial danger to life in or around the lake because, it was assumed, the tailings would mix with water to form a fluid discharge more dense than lake water. This discharge would not mix with the lake water itself but would flow along the bottom of the great trough (600-900 feet deep) to its lowest point and remain there.[10]

Reserve achieved full operation in 1963. It was an enormous effort requiring the investment of over $350 million and resulting directly or indirectly in the employment of 3,300 people. At full operation, the processing plant produced approximately 30,000 tons of pelletized iron each day, using 500,000 gallons of water per minute to dispose of almost 67,000 tons of tailings per day. In just 12 days the "sediment" contributed by Reserve equaled that contributed to Lake Superior by all U.S. tributary streams in one year.[11]

Reserve has become increasingly profitable. In 1973-74 the daily profit of Reserve was about $60,000 per day. This was a 90% return on owners' equity.[12] This means that for every dollar Armco and Republic initially invested they enjoyed a return of 90 cents—and this was just in one year.

Things went fine for Reserve until 1969 when a report issued in Washington accused Reserve of seriously polluting the water of Lake Superior. This report was to launch a major investigation into the activities of Reserve. On April 28, 1971, Environmental Protection Agency administrator William Ruckelshaus notified Reserve that it was in violation of federal and state water quality standards.[13] Reserve was given 180 days to effect compliance with these standards. Reserve failed to respond to the request, and on February 2, 1972 the Department of Justice filed suit against Reserve in the U.S. District Court in Minnesota. Thus began a long, complex, costly legal battle aimed at making Reserve comply with the appropriate environmental standards.

One of the primary issues in this litigation was whether or not the tiny asbestos fibers which came from Reserve's discharge were a severe health threat to the population of Duluth and the surrounding areas. It was established at the trial that if asbestos fibers are inhaled in sufficient quantity, they cause cancer. However, the asbestos fibers were in the drinking water of the residents of Duluth, and the current medical science could not be sure of the effects of the fibers in this medium. Whether or not the threat to health was sufficient to justify closing Reserve until it could dispose of its waste elsewhere is the focus of the litigation. This litigation is over 6 years old and the resolution is not final. To this date (Spring, 1978) Reserve continues to discharge 67,000 tons of waste (containing asbestos fibers) per day into Lake Superior and the fines or penalties it has had to pay are minimal relative to the profits received. The most recent record of the case indicates that the court having jurisdiction in the case moved the date when it would order Reserve to cease discharging effluent into the lake from July 7, 1977 until April 15, 1980.[14]

Reserve and its owners Armco and Republic have battled the plaintiffs— the city of Duluth, other cities, the states of Minnesota, Wisconsin and Michigan, the federal government, the environmental groups—every inch of the way. During the initial trial, representatives of Reserve argued that they could modify the lake discharge method to satisfy environmental standards. They argued this in spite of the fact their own studies had concluded modification was not feasible. When the trial judge found this out, he became enraged and in a statement which characterizes much of the Reserve ligitation said:

> The court has stated on the record and will repeat here that Reserve's insistence on advocating the underwater disposal system which has been deemed infeasible by one of its owners and the failure to timely produce the documents dealing with possible on-land disposal systems has substantially delayed the outcome of this litigation in a situation where a speedy resolution is essential. . .
>
> Even when faced with the evidence in this case that their discharge creates a substantial threat to the health of the people exposed to it, defendants are reluctant to curtail their discharge until the latest possible moment, presumably in order to prolong the profitability of the present discharge.
>
> The testimony adduced at trial was to the effect that (with product improvement) Reserve, Republic and Armco could afford *at the very least* a $180,000,000 to $200,000,000 capital outlay with reasonably associated operating costs without substantially changing their economic situation as to profitability, intraindustry position, interest coverage, bond rating, etc. This figure should come as no shock to the defendants. Their own documents recently discovered support this fact.[15]

At 12:01 a.m., April 2, 1974, Reserve was ordered closed by Judge Lord, who wrote the opinion quoted from above. This order was appealed and not quite two days later the Eighth Circuit Court of Appeals suspended this order pending a full hearing by the Circuit Court. The most recent court order gives Reserve until 1980—a full 10 years after it was notified it was in violation of law, to conform to environmental standards. A final development which is noteworthy in this context was the removal of Judge Lord from the case by his superiors in the Eighth Circuit because they believed he had demonstrated judicial prejudice. Judge Lord was on the case from the beginning and was the closest "objective" person to the presentation of the evidence. The Eighth Circuit said in its order of removal:

> . . . the trial judge announced on the record that witnesses called by Reserve could not be believed, that in every instance Reserve Mining Company hid the evidence, misrepresented, delayed and frustrated the ultimate conclusions and that he did not have "any faith" in witnesses to be called by Reserve.[16]

The record above reveals a picture of a large corporate enterprise managed, we must assume, by individuals who care about human welfare. Why then does the record demonstrate that Reserve *could* act to lessen the threat to health and the environment without threatening its competitive position but has not?

What circumstances are there in this rather complex case which might explain how the managers of Reserve could, in good conscience, reconcile their behavior on behalf of Reserve with the damage to the environment? Consider these questions:

1. Who owns Reserve? Who owns the owners? Do you know of any effective way in which the owners of Reserve's owners might organize to control the behavior of Reserve?
2. What product does Reserve make? Are the consumers of this product likely to act in a way which would force Reserve to develop a solution for the threat it poses?
3. What happens to the product made by Reserve? When consumers, you and I, and other individual human consumers, ultimately gain access to Reserve's product is it in a form that would enable us to recognize it as Reserve's product so that we could refrain from buying it to express our dissatisfaction with Reserve?
4. Given the information above, how does the conventional wisdom explain the business conduct of Reserve?
5. The management of Reserve must meet well defined standards of performance. What are these standards? Or, is there only one standard and from this one are all others derived?

Is Reserve unique or does it represent a general pattern of commercial behavior? A second case involving one of the largest and most successful American corporations may suggest conduct like Reserve's is not unique.

FORD MOTOR COMPANY

In our national effort to solve common problems caused by our private choices we have spent too much time on moralistic and ideological disputes and too little time seeking practical compromises. Our real task is to find the best balance between benefits to people as citizens and costs to people as consumers.
(Quote of Henry Ford II from "The High Cost of Regulation," *Newsweek*, p. 15, March 20, 1978.)

The Ford Motor Company designed, produced and marketed the Pinto automobile beginning in 1970. The gas tank in the Pinto was located behind the rear axle; it was only 3¼ inches behind the differential housing.[17] In rear-end collisions the gas tank would be pushed into the differential housing which would work like a can opener on the tank. Ford Motor Company produced a movie for its own use which showed a Pinto backing into a wall at 20 miles per hour. In the film the gas tank of the car ruptured with such force, according to one observer, that "it looked like a fireman had stuck a hose inside the car and turned it on." Apparently the gas tank was shoved into the housing which split the tank and literally threw the liquid substance into the passenger compartment. The location of the tank was not substantially changed until 1977.

In 1971 Lily Gray was driving a Pinto with Richard Grimshaw riding as a passenger. The car stalled on the freeway and was struck from behind by another car. Lily Gray died of burns suffered when the passenger compartment exploded in flames and Grimshaw was burned over 90% of his body; he required over 60 operations in the next seven years to repair some of the damage done.

Grimshaw and a representative of the estate of Lily Gray sued Ford. The trial was held in late 1977. After the evidence was heard a jury returned for the plaintiffs the largest single award of damages in U.S. history. It awarded Grimshaw $3.5 million to compensate him for his injury and $125 million in punitive damages. The punitive damage award was so large that after the trial, the judge proposed reducing the award to $6.3 million. At this date, Grimshaw is prepared to accept this, but Ford may still appeal.

Observers explained that the reason for this large punitive damage award was the fact that the evidence at the trial made it clear that Ford management knew of the dangerous tank design and produced the car anyway. One juror commented that, "Ford knew people would be killed."

It appears that Ford carefully assessed the savings which would result from this particular design. Ford's own documents revealed that Ford management calculated they could save $20.9 million if they delayed making gas tank alterations for two years. Also, the cost of the possible lawsuits could be calculated and then set against the projected savings. From the testimony at the Grimshaw trial it appears another juror reasoned that Ford could have saved as much as $100 million by not installing safer tanks which would have cost $10 to $15 more per car. Some of the jurors reasoned that to punish Ford, the punitive damage award should exceed the total savings resulting from the gas tank design. Thus, the jury settled on $125 million.

It is estimated that Ford will report 1977 fourth quarter profits of from $380 million to $395 million. The jury's punitive damage award is about equal to one month's profit for Ford.

Again, consider this question: how can one understand how Ford could consciously calculate and weigh the dangers of the gas tank design against the money costs of changing the design and opt for lowest cost?

How can this behavior be considered socially responsible or desirable? Consider the possible answers to these questions:

1. Do you think the engineers who designed the location for the gas tank and the tank itself and who presumably knew better than anyone the consequences of this design made the decision to use that particular design? (It appears from the reports of the Grimshaw trial that at least one Ford engineer was a critic of the Pinto fuel tank design.)
2. In what way can those in Ford who are responsible for the adoption of the Pinto fuel tank design be held accountable for this decision. Should they be held accountable?
3. In this case what standards are to be used to define "reasonably prudent" behavior of management? (To adopt an analogy from tort law, one may not be held liable for negligence if he or she is acting as a reasonably prudent person would under the circumstances.)
4. Assume that the large award of punitive damages is not altered on appeal. Who ultimately would bear the cost of the punitive damage

award assuming that the prices of automobiles are not subject to substantial competitive market conditions? Are there market inducements for socially desirable behavior? Trace the effects of this payment. Who, ultimately will bear the cost of this penalty?

CONFRONTING THE MODERN CORPORATION

The traditional, individual-centered model of a market economy used to explain and understand how goods and services are distributed in this country has failed to account for some significant activity of the modern corporate enterprise. This failure has been recognized by many. However, the response has been to enact enormous amounts of federal legislation applicable to business conduct. Most of this legislation focuses on corporate conduct and does not address the central problem of the manner in which today's significant corporate sellers make decisions.

The image we must focus on in constructing a social theory (and legislation) for confronting the less desirable effects of the large corporate enterprise upon our society is one based upon the reality of the current decision making process of the largest 200 corporations. More precisely, we must focus on the fact that significant corporate decisions are made in a corporate board room in which sit 15 to 25 individuals looking at sheets of paper upon which numerous figures portray the outcomes of many possible choices. These sheets of paper are summaries of other long and complex reports generated as the result of meetings at the lower divisional or subsidiary level; and the people in these meetings discuss reports from the departmental level, etc. In almost every instance involving a matter of choice, the more profitable alternative is favored. By the time the issues are presented to the body which has the legal responsibility for managing the corporation (the board of directors) many alternatives have already been evaluated and excluded. Because the information reaching the board has been carefully selected at each level with a view toward the most profitable alternative and because the board is substantially removed from the market and the production facility, the board will almost always opt for the more profitable alternative. How else can one explain the conduct of Reserve and Ford?

A reasonable solution would be based upon altering the information flow within these large corporations so that the decisional structure of the corporation would more closely conform to the perspective of the rational decision-maker in the conventional model. Responsible behavior begins with perception. The responsible person observes and accounts for phenomena the irresponsible person ignores.[18]

There have been a number of suggestions for changing corporate perception. However, only the one cogently advanced by Professor Christopher Stone of the University of Southern California Law School in his book, *Where the Law Ends*, seems to confront the image of corporate decision making which we should be concerned about. Professor Stone suggests federal legislation to alter the structure of the board of directors of large corporations. He recommends:

1. Interested or inside directors—those who have a position with management—should be eliminated in corporations of major impact, i.e., corporations over $50 million in sales;
2. A percentage of the board (either two persons or 10% of the directors, whichever is larger) could neither personally own stock nor be a director or officer of a firm that owned shares in the company.
3. The functions of directors should be defined and standards for holding directors liable for neglect of duty should be developed.
4. Directors should be given a full time staff accountable to them and not management. This staff should take steps to assure the directors get all relevant information on a choice confronting the board.

In addition to the above Stone would require by federal law the selection of General Public Directors (GPD's) and Special Public Directors (SPD's). Every manufacturing corporation would have to have 10% of its directors be GPD's for every billion dollars in sales or assets. This means the 14 largest corporations would have all GPD's. GPD's would be selected not by shareholders but by a Federal Corporation Commission or, perhaps, an agency like S.E.C. and would have, among others, the following duties:

1. to check corporate compliance with all applicable federal and state laws;
2. to serve as a monitor on internal information and other systems;
3. to serve as a "hot line" to employees who have vital information;
4. to prepare impact studies on proposed major corporate actions; and,
5. in general, be "probing and vigilant."

Corporations engaged in a critical area of social concern—those depending upon rapid technological innovation the impact of which is difficult to assess; or those which are likely to pollute or affect the physical or social environment—would be assigned SPD's. SPD's are directors who have special backgrounds or training in science, foreign affairs, etc. If a corporation is delinquent or in violation of some federal regulatory agency's rules, a SPD would be assigned to bring about reform from within.

These proposals may seem drastic but the remedy must be in direct proportion to the threat posed. The examples of Reserve and Ford show the threat is substantial. The threat is all the more insidious when one realizes we have no established social ideology to explain the paradox presented in the first portion of this chapter. The corporation has replaced the *individual* (human) as a significant seller but the entire elaborate social ideology (primarily economics and law) still assume individuals are the primary actors in our society. At the very least, we should begin, as students of economics, law and business conduct, to focus on the less desirable impact of our society of its predominant institution, the modern corporation.

ENDNOTES

1. J. Galbraith, The Affluent Society (1958).
2. *Id.*, at 9 (3rd ed.).

3. *See* Friedman, *A Friedman Doctrine: The Social Responsibility of Business Is To Increase Its Profits,* N.Y. Times, Sept. 13, 1970 (Magazine) at 32; and **M. Friedmen, Capitalism and Freedom.** (1962).
4. **Galbraith,** *supra* note 1, at 11 (3rd ed.).
5. **A. Smith, An Inquiry into the Nature and Causes of the Wealth of Nations,** 1776, (R. Campbell and A. Skinner ed.) (1976) Vol. 1 at 9-10 of the General Introduction.
6. *Id.* at 10.
7. **P. Samuelson, Economics, An Introductory Analysis,** 41 (7th ed., 1967). There are parts of this text devoted to a discussion of corporations, but none contradict the point illustrated by the quote.
8. The "harmless sand" characterization comes from a source I was unable to locate but was cited in, Eagen, The Enforcement of Anti-Pollution Regulations with Special Consideration of The Reserve Mining Case, an unpublished paper read at the Annual Convention of the American Business Law Association, at Miami, Florida, August 22, 1977.
9. **E. Schaumburg, Judgment Reserved, A Landmark Environmental Case,** 47 (1976).
10. *Id.,* at 47-48.
11. *Id.,* at 69, citing, The Stoddard Report, a federal governmental report on the influence of taconite tailings on the water quality of Lake Superior, 1968.
12. United States v. Reserve Mining Company, 380 F Supp. 11, 19 (D. Minn. 1974).
13. **Schaumburg,** *supra,* note 9 at 147.
14. **Environmental Reports,** Current Developments, 164 (June 3, 1977).
15. 380 F Supp. at 18-19 (1974).
16. 44 LW 2306 (1976) citing transcript of November 14, 1975 hearings at 2-5, 56 and 109.
17. These facts and those that follow were taken from, *Why the Pinto Jury Felt Ford Deserved $125 Million Penalty,* Wall St. Journal, Feb. 14, 1978, at 1.
18. This thought and the solution herein proposed are based upon, **C. Stone, Where The Law Ends — The Social Control of Corporate Behavior,** 1976. Stone is also responsible for the observation that our law ignores or has failed to develop principles of liability holding corporate management personally accountable for their decisions. The reasons for this, he argues, are that law has traditionally focused on humans as primary actors in our society, not on corporations.

6

On Having One's Cake

Bill Shaw*

My dad used to tell a story of a man who claimed to have resolved the ancient dilemma of having his cake and eating it too. It seems, however, that this fellow blended his philosophical pursuits with a note of enterprise and larceny as well. He would consume the cake whole, immediately, and fresh from the oven! Upon being quizzed regarding this most crucial point of his performance, and the least defensible, the culprit would reply with alarming innocence, "Hell, I never said my solution was perfect."

Well, if his answer wasn't perfect, it worked perfectly enough to suit him— once per sucker. Dad never explained what happened to his onetime friend, but unless I miss my guess he's still alive and well—and working for the utility company.

Utility companies are taking a bad rap nowadays—from customers who complain that rates are too high and services are inadequate (especially during cold winter months) and from environmentalists who complain that utilities are raping the land, stripping it of limited resources (coal, oil, uranium), and subjecting all of us to serious pollution hazards. Not many people are willing to do without jobs and services however, and it is quite likely that these companies will continue to operate as long as they can do so at a profit. Now who's the villain?

In this brief chapter perhaps we can analyze the horns of this dilemma, examine some of the trade-offs or policy decisions that must be made, and see what role the law plays in this process. In an attempt to illustrate these points it will be helpful to focus on a federal statute and a recent court decision that is now in the process of appeal to the U.S. Supreme Court.

*University of Texas at Austin

THE CLEAN AIR ACT

For our purposes we need go back in time no further than 1970 to gain some insights into air pollution problems that are confronting us today. The 1970 Clean Air Act[1] gave the Environmental Protection Agency (EPA) power to set primary health standards and secondary welfare standards for certain pollutants in the ambient (surrounding) air. With some adjustments, the primary standards were to be achieved by mid-1975 and the secondary standards within a reasonable period of time.

The main task of protecting and enhancing air quality was delegated to the states. The role of EPA was to approve and supervise state implementation plans (SIP's) that met certain criteria. Stationary sources of pollution—utility plants, factories, mills—were the chief targets of state efforts. Following a public hearing, permits requiring the use of control technology (stack scrubbers) or other means of curbing pollution could be issued. Penalties for permit violation were stiff, but a stationary source could be granted a variance if the SIP itself was not jeopardized.

While the states were mainly concerned with stationary sources, their efforts were to be joined and supplemented on a second front. Congress also required a 90% roll-back in hydrocarbon and carbon monoxide emissions from mobile sources of pollution by 1975. The auto industry was successful in getting a two year suspension of this deadline, but that simply meant that states were required to redouble their efforts to make up the difference and still meet the deadlines.

The combined lobbying efforts of big business and big labor to forestall pollution control made itself felt beyond the confines of Washington D.C. and Detroit. The economy may have received a boost, but the tough job of dealing with the nation's air pollution was taken back a notch.

Speaking to The National Association of Regional Councils of Government in 1975, Russell Train, Administrator of the Environmental Protection Agency, evaluated the success of emission control efforts as follows:

> . . . the first major deadline under the Clean Air Act for the achievement of health-related standards for six serious pollutants—will fall only a few days from now, on Saturday, May 31. We will have achieved, on a national level, none of these standards. We will, on the other hand, have accomplished—both nationally and in major areas of the country—some rather deep reductions in some air pollutants and put in motion the basic machinery we must have to continue to lighten the load of hazardous air pollutants in the air we breathe.

Recent amendments to the Clean Air Act[2] follow the same basic structure as their predecessor. States have until January 1, 1979, to submit for EPA approval new SIP's that are to go into effect by July 1, 1979. Air quality standards are to be achieved by December 31, 1982, but EPA may grant an extension until 1987 for photochemical (smog producing) oxidants and carbon monoxide.

In those Air Quality Control Regions (A.Q.C.R.) within a state that are not currently meeting national standards (non-attainment areas), new sources of air pollution—plants, factories, and mills—cannot be licensed unless each applicant firm can demonstrate that it will reduce emissions of the offending pollutant by an amount greater than that which it will add. This means that the applicant will have to close down or restrict similar operations of its own or receive binding cut-back commitments from other firms. The latter alternative has given rise to an active market in pollution rights.

When the new SIP's go into effect July 1, 1979, those firms that want to expand their present operations as well as those that want to open additional facilities must not jeopardize further reasonable progress toward air quality standards. Although Congress granted the auto industry a further extension in the 1977 amendments, cleaner cars should be in production in time to contribute to the achievement of the December 31, 1982 deadline.

ANALYSIS OF THE CLEAN AIR ACT

Consider the basic policy-making features of The Clean Air Act and its recent amendments. Congress was called upon to weigh and balance environmental quality v. jobs and profits. The judgment of Congress on such matters can be revised from time to time (if Congress acts in a constitutional manner). Since legislators operate on imperfect knowledge just as all of us do, their decisions with short-and long-run implications need constant attention.

The question is *where to make a stand?* How clean is clean enough? Since we have limited resources to allocate among socially desirable projects, how are priorities to be determined? On paper at least, Congress has decided that *public health* is the bottom line, but repeated postponements call into question the practicality and the wisdom of that decision.

Perhaps the 1975 deadline was simply an unrealistic objective from the beginning. If the failure to attain it has increased our resolve, then it is quite possible that the knowledge and experience gained can be used with great advantage on the next effort. A too ambitious goal runs the risk of failure and a general demoralization, but it can move us beyond all expectations as well.

If Congress acted in good faith by establishing such a tight schedule to begin with, was Congress correct in its judgment that people value health, for example, over a steady job? Recent events in Pennsylvania and Ohio indicate that some voters prefer to run the risk of environmentally related illness rather than to see their job opportunities diminished by expenditures on additional pollution controls. This preference may not indicate a lack of concern about health, however. It may only indicate the voters' belief that the point of diminishing returns on control technology has been exceeded and that other aspects of the human environment should be advanced. However the vote is interpreted, it is clear evidence that policymakers cannot expect their judgment to be accepted uncritically.

NUCLEAR ENERGY

The Price-Anderson Act,[3] first enacted in 1957 and amended as recently as 1975, placed a ceiling of $560,000,000.00 on the aggregate liability for a single nuclear accident.[4] Out of this fund all personal injury and property damage claims must be settled; it must support the costs of investigating claims and defending damage suits as well.

Keep in mind that the $560,000,000 is mainly U.S. taxpayers' money. Only a part of it comes out of a utility company's pocket. The Act requires each firm to obtain up to $125,000,000 private insurance coverage. The remaining amount is insured by Uncle Sam at "token" premium rates. Federal subsidization is being phased out, but the maximum liability per accident remains the same.

Proponents of the limited liability stipulated in Price-Anderson argue that without it, nuclear powered utilities would not be built. However, in a significant 1977 district court decision, *Carolina Environmental Study Group v. Atomic Energy Commission*,[5] the limited liability provisions of Price-Anderson were declared unconstitutional. While an impressive debate on reactor safety raged between pro-nuclear forces (those who rallied in support of AEC's optimistic safety study[6]) and their gloomy detractors, the court itself was un-moved:

> The case can concern itself too much with the mathematical odds for or against a particular nuclear catastrophe of a particular dimension. The question is not whether a nuclear catastrophe (at two hundred to one or twenty thousand to one) is more or less likely than a tornado, an earthquake or a collision with a comet; the significant conclusion is that under the odds quoted by either side, a nuclear catastrophe is a real, not fanciful, possibility.

> The court finds . . . that a core melt at McGuire or Catawba can reasonably be expected to produce hundreds or thousands of fatalities, numerous illnesses, genetic effects of unpredictable degree and nature for succeeding generations, thyroid ailments and cancers in numerous people, damage to other life and widespread damage to property. Areas as large as several thousand square miles might be contaminated and require evacuation. Since life of individual human beings, as shown in a number of publicized cases involving death or disability is now being valued in some cases as sums greatly exceeding a million dollars, it would not require death or a serious injury to many people to exceed the $560,000,000 Price-Anderson Act limitation now in effect. Nor, in a day when failure of an earthen dam in sparsely populated Idaho can produce property damage reported by the press at about a billion dollars, is it unreasonable to conclude, as I do, that radioactive pollution of a few hundred square miles of heavily populated Piedmont, North Carolina or South Carolina could well produce property damage vastly exceeding the Price-Anderson ceiling.[7]

The offending provisions of Price-Anderson were found to be in violation of the Due Process Clause of The Fifth Amendment and the equal protection provision that is included within it.[8] Regarding due process considerations, the court found that the limited amount of recovery was not rationally related to the magnitude of potential losses. It tended to encourage short-cuts and irresponsibility in safety and environmental matters. Finally, there was no *quid pro quo* for limited liability—no legitimate exchange of trade-off of burdens and benefits. Those who engage in intrinsically ultrahazardous activity are normally held strictly liable for the harm they cause. The Price-Anderson Act simply confirms the strict liability status of ultrahazardous nuclear facilities and gives them limited financial responsibility to boot. Potential victims receive nothing in return; Price-Anderson is a one way street.

Equal protection provisions are offended because the Price-Anderson ceiling unreasonably places the cost of a widespread social benefit (abundant and relatively inexpensive electric power) on an arbitrarily chosen segment of the population (those who live in the vicinity of the nuclear generator and are likely to be injured by a nuclear catastrophe). According to District Court Judge McMillan, who decided the case, this feature of the Act is quite unnecessary. The public good can be served just as well without it.

ANALYSIS OF THE *CAROLINA STUDY* DECISION

Full liability could be spread among all power companies building or operating nuclear generators. If utility rates increased as the insurance expense was passed along to customers, this would do no more than place nuclear power on a par with its competitors—coal, oil and gas fired utilities. If nonnuclear utilities must assume full responsibility for their conduct, why should not nuclear utilities be required to do the same? Further, if the result is nuclear fuel's loss of a competitive price edge over coal and others, isn't that simply what one should expect from the operation of the free market system?

If the U.S. government refuses to provide subsidized insurance protection at low rates and withdraws the $560 million liability ceiling (i.e., if the Supreme Court upholds the *Carolina Study* case and Congress fails to revise the offending provision of the Price-Anderson Act), utility firms will be forced to insure privately. This will compel such firms to account for or to internalize the full cost of their operations, including the social cost that they are now imposing on nearby residents. Like fossil fuel plants that are required by the Clean Air Act to spend huge sums to reduce harmful emissions, nuclear facilities may be forced to bear full financial responsibility for the harm imposed on others. These costs will be passed along to consumers in the form of higher utility rates, but at least the consumers—rather than U.S. taxpayers at large—will be picking up the tab for nuclear powered generating plants.

Former U.S. Senator Tunney of California estimated that the cost of $500 million private insurance coverage would be $500,000 per year. That would be approximately one-tenth of a mill per kilowatt hour for a 1000 megawatt nuclear power plant.[9] If the ceiling on liability is lifted, rates would have to be calculated on losses in the billions, but Senator Tunney's figures at least give a first approximation of the added expense consumers would be forced to bear.

CONCLUSION

In the Clean Air Act and Price-Anderson examples, you can see the fine balance between environmental, health, and safety considerations and those of full employment, cheap energy, and an expanding economy. No single solution will satisfy all parties; nor is it possible for either side to have its way

completely. Compromise—that classic escape from the horns of a dilemma—
is an uninspiring model.

You will be quick to see that only pure artifice allows the problem to be
treated as if two sides alone existed—there are hundreds of different views and
they can't be nicely categorized pro-environment v. pro-development. The
most ardent nuclear power proponent wants a safe environment and the most
out-spoken environmentalist realizes that his material needs will make some
demands on limited natural resources.

It is the law that mediates these competing demands. Legal and political
institutions—the executive, legislative, and judicial branches of government—
are the chief instruments in formulating and implementing policy.

They do not operate in a vacuum, however. If they are to function effectively, they must be attuned to informed opinion and they must be sensitive to the
elaborate ramifications of their decisions. A victory for oil interests off the
Atlantic coast can mean trouble for the fishing industry. Protection of the
snail darter, endangered by the Tellico Dam, can mean the loss of millions
of tax dollars sunk in a useless structure. A plant that must spend millions
on emission control equipment may be forced to dismiss employees with
families to support. The subtle and intricate interplay of cause and effect is
sometimes demoralizing, sometimes tragic.

The Clean Air Act and the Price-Anderson Act are legislative attempts to
adjust (one might as well say *juggle*) thousands of competing interests. The
executive branch must shoulder the enforcement task, frequently with the
assistance of a specially equipped administrative agency. From time to time
the judiciary is called upon to interpret statutes and to declare their constitutionality.

These great legal institutions are merely the superstructure, however. As a
rule the people who make them work know very little about the chemistry of
the air pollution or the complexities of nuclear fission. Judges, legislators, administrators, prosecutors, and defense counsel—all of these have to be informed by experts from many different disciplines. And the task does not
end there. Lawmakers cannot function effectively if they are out of touch with
consumers, business people, laborers, and other special interests.

In sum, the task of pollution control is just one aspect of a broader challenge. The *human environment* is more intricate by far than the physical environment alone. It consists of our culture and life-style woven from the values
and spirit of the people.

No great surprise, then, to find that solutions are hard to come by. Legal
institutions are only human, fallible institutions. Sometimes a middle way
is all they have to offer.

And if that is insufficient, perhaps you should meet a beguiling philosopher
my father knew . . .

END NOTES

1. 42 USCA § 7401 *et seq.* (as amended 1977, formerly 42 USCA § 1857 *et seq.* 1970)
2. *Ibid.*

3. 42 U.S.C. § 2210(e)
4. One other provision of the act § 2210 (o), allows payment beyond this limit
    . . . if, upon petition and showing, a cognizant United States district court determines that a particular incident has produced losses that exceed the $560,000,000 limit of liability: (1) payments going beyond 15% of that limit ($84,000,000) may not be made without court approval; (2) payments above 15% must be under a plan of distribution or found to be not prejudicial to the subsequent adoption of such a plan; (3) claims for later discovered and future injuries must be provided for; and (4) all further distribution must be determined by the district judge.
5. 431 F. Supp. 203 (1977).
6. The Reactor Safety Study was sponsored by the U.S. Atomic Energy Commission to estimate the public risks that could be involved in potential accidents in commercial nuclear power plants of the type now in use. It was performed under the independent direction of Professor Norman C. Rasmussen of the Massachusetts Institute of Technology. The risks had to be estimated, rather than measured, because although there are about 50 such plants now operating, there have been no nuclear accidents to date. The methods used to develop these estimates are based on those developed by the Department of Defense and the National Aeronautics and Space Administration in the last 10 years.

    The objective of the study was to make a realistic estimate of these risks and to compare with non-nuclear risks to which our society and its individuals are already exposed. This information helps to determine the future use of nuclear power as a source of electricity.

    The basic conclusion of this study is that the risks to the public from potential accidents in nuclear power plants are very small.

    Reactor Safety Study: An Assessment of Accident Risks in U.S. Commercial Nuclear Power Plants, 16 **Atomic Energy Law Review** 177 (1974).
7. 431 F. Supp. at 214-215.
8. Bolling v. Sharpe, 347 US 497 (1954).
9. **Report by the Joint Committee on Atomic Energy, Amendments to the Price-Anderson provisions of the Atomic Energy Act of 1954,** S. Rep. No. 96-454, 94th Cong. 1st Sess. 30-31 (1975).

Part III

Business Law

All the chapters of Part III deal to some extent with the substantive law of business relationships, but the emphasis on business activities varies dramatically from chapter to chapter. No chapter merely describes what business people must do to protect themselves. That is not the main thrust of "business law" as our authors perceive it. Rather, they recognize that business and law are subsystems of our society, that business participants have duties as well as rights, and that business and law have a symbiotic relationship.

Within this framework of common views, individual authors deal with specific aspects of business law. Some authors describe and evaluate legislation or elements of the common law. Some question the sufficiency of legal theory or acquaint us with revealing historical developments. One deals mainly with family relationships in which business law is incidental. In so doing, he reminds us that the principles of law transcend business affairs and that business law is representative of law in general.

Part III opens with two topics of general interest. In Chapter 7, Professor Elliot explains the rights and duties of parents and infants in our society, and he describes the "overseeing eye of the state." Professor Myers, in Chapter 8, discusses the American rule concerning the awarding of attorneys' fees to winning litigants. That chapter reveals some important implications for the future of public interest litigation.

Chapters 9 and 10 focus on regulatory theory and on the history of corporate disclosure regulation. In Chapter 9, Professor Brennan comments on the relative worth of legal and economic theory in antitrust regulation, and he draws an illustration from the cement industry. Professor Wiesen then discribes some major trends in corporate disclosure regulation engaged in by the Securities Exchange Commission.

The next four chapters present topics of substantive business law. Professor Reed, in Chapter 11, discusses the approach of the Federal Trade Commission to the regulation of advertising. This chapter discusses the Commission's early history, some examples of deceptive advertising, and several important trends in advertising regulation.

Professor Allison's chapter covers the "private law" of competition. Professor Allison discusses competitive practices which cross traditional boundaries of reasonable and ethical behavior: trade disparagement, false representations, trademark infringements, and misappropriation of trade secrets.

Professor Jentz, in Chapter 13, explains the purpose, coverage, and enforcement provisions of the Occupational Safety and Health Act, and he comments on problems associated with that Act. Professor Naffziger presents, in Chapter 14, a survey of important legislation dealing with discrimination in employment. In discussing the Civil Rights Act and its amendments, he examines some significant social and legal issues.

The book ends with Professor Hewitt's comment on the meaning, history, and current importance of franchising. His chapter brings to a fitting close this collection of commentary on the developing fabric of business law.

7

Rights and Responsibilities Of Infants and Their Parents

by William G. Elliott*

This chapter examines the relationship of infants and their parents and presents the legal rights and responsibilities of each in our society. Quite frequently when these subjects arise in the basic undergraduate law course, an opportunity for discussion does not exist because of time limitations and other curriculum demands. What follows is a compilation of topics and concerns students most frequently raise regarding infants and parents. The subject matter has been organized so as to concentrate upon infants' rights and responsibilities as these relate to contracts, torts, crimes, delinquency, guardianship and bastardy questions. This is followed by a discussion of parent and child relationships relating to care, custody, control, support, schooling and shared responsibility for infants' torts and crimes.

RIGHTS AND RESPONSIBILITIES OF INFANTS

A person is considered an infant from birth until he or she attains the statutory age of majority, which is usually in the late teens. As an infant, a person is treated with tender regard by the law, which acts to protect the infant more than an adult. States have statutes which prohibit the sale to infants of alcohol, drugs, cigarettes and other products considered dangerous to health. There are statutes protecting morals of infants. There are employment laws prohibiting infants from working in hazardous jobs, or requiring work permits that usually may not be issued to infants younger than fourteen. There are statutes designed to protect infants from recklessly spending their money. Others limit the ability of infants to purchase or dispose of real property until reaching majority. And there are statutes which limit infants' responsibility in the commission of crimes, torts and the execution of contracts. Where

*Saginaw Valley State College

the infant is not specifically protected by law, his or her rights and responsibilities are identical to those of adults.

STATE CONTROL AND INTEREST

The ultimate control of an infant reposes with the state. The state may assume direction as well as control of an infant to insure that the infant's rights are fully protected, even to the exclusion of the parents' wishes. The state's power is exercised through a subdivision of the local county court's equity system.

The best interest of the infant is the critical question in all cases of control. Right of control will remain with the natural parents unless they prove incapable. Should parental incapability be shown, then control will be taken over by the state and passed on to a competent relative or third party. Consultation with the infant for his or her preference usually is part of the determination process, especially in those instances where the infant is mature enough to exercise sound judgment. The court also relies on testimony of parents, relatives, neighbors, social workers and others in order to arrive at a decision in the best interest of the infant.

INFANTS' CONTRACTS

Because of society's desire to protect infants' estates, special rules have been developed that restrict their ability to contract during infancy. Generally contracts they execute are voidable until shortly after majority. They are voidable by the infant but not by the other contracting party, unless such other party is also an infant. The degree of performance of the contractual duties affects whether the infant subsequently will be bound after attaining majority. If the contract is wholly executory, the infant is not bound unless he or she performs some act of affirmance after his or her majority. If the contract is wholly executed, it is binding until disaffirmance which must take place soon after majority. If the contract is partially executory and partially executed, the infant must disaffirm in order not to be bound. Disaffirmance generally can be made at any time during the infancy or soon after attaining majority. Affirmance can occur only after the attainment of majority.

Not all contracts executed by infants are voidable. In contracts involving necessities, infants are liable for the reasonable value of necessities which have not otherwise been supplied to the infants. And while infants may not be able to contract for other goods and services, they can act as agents for adults and enter into contracts that are binding on the principal-adults.

INFANTS' TORTS

Infants can be civilly liable for the torts they commit after the attainment of a certain age, usually seven years. Prior to attainment of such age they are presumed incapable of tort because they do not possess the required mental or physical capacity. However, once achieving the requisite capacities, which increasingly are assumed to be present as the infant approaches adulthood, the infant is subject to the entire array of tort actions such as assault, negligence, and wrongful death, and may be held liable for damages suffered by injured parties. Infants also may be the victims of torts by adults or other infants, and infants of any age can recover damages for their loss.

INFANTS' CRIME

Just as in tort, infants can be liable for crimes they commit after the attainment of a certain age, usually seven years. Prior to that age they conclusively are presumed incapable of crime because they lack the capacity of felonious intent. Between the ages of seven and fourteen an infant is presumed to lack capacity. This presumption is rebuttable. After age fourteen, an infant usually is presumed capable of committing a crime and may be subject to treatment as an adult in the criminal court.

Each state has statutory procedures for the prosecution of infants under the jurisdiction of the juvenile court. The majority of jurisdictions also provide that older infants may be tried for crimes in the court of general criminal jurisdiction, applying adult regulations for bail, trial, judgment and sentence. However, modern law does not require that infants be treated as adults in most criminal actions. Thus, special rules and regulations befitting the youthful offender have been devised and are concerned more with rehabilitation than punishment of the infant.

JUVENILES AND DELINQUENCY

States have passed special statutory regulations in response to the need to protect, correct, and discipline infants who are delinquent or neglected and dependent. These statutes provide for intervention by the state in cases of abandoned, neglected, delinquent, and incorrigible infants as well as for those who are incapable of self-support because of age, physical, and mental incapacities.

Custody or commitment is not considered penal in nature, but it is accomplished instead by a civil proceeding initiated by the state for the collective welfare of the infant and society. The proceeding is held without a jury, before a judge who is to act as a substitute parent and render a decision for the child's improved well-being.

The proceedings for custody or commitment of a dependent or delinquent infant are conducted in a juvenile court. It may be a court of record, but for protection of the infant, records usually are not available to the general public. Whether custody or commitment should be ordered is a question of fact which the court determines in light of the circumstances and statutes. The statutes are construed strictly in instances involving freedom of the infant's movements, but liberally when the question is the infant's welfare. Thus a juvenile court disposes of all cases in the best interest of the dependent or delinquent infant, with the duration of custody or commitment being designed to achieve that end.

Statutes treating infant acts which would otherwise be crimes except for the age of the perpetrator are called juvenile delinquency statutes. The infants who fall within these statutes are considered juvenile delinquents. Under some state statutes, infants who are nearly adults may be subject to both juvenile and penal criminal statutes. In instances of dual qualification, a hearing is conducted before the juvenile tribunal where the decision might be to waive juvenile jurisdiction and treat the infant as an adult. In such cases, the important consideration is the age of the juvenile at the time of the hearing rather than the age of the juvenile at the time of the act.

GUARDIANSHIP OF INFANTS

Guardianship is a trust relationship of the highest character, in which an adult guardian acts for the infant, known as a ward. The guardianship may be established for overseeing an estate, funds, a lawsuit, or the care, custody and control of the ward.

The appointment of a guardian usually is within the sole discretion of the court, which is free to consider the desires of the parent, the spouse, or the ward. In most cases the court will appoint a near relative adult who is competent and suitable and who does not possess an adverse interest to the ward. The guardian is given reasonable payment for services and is reimbursed for expenses after submitting a billing to the court for approval.

As noted previously, infants may sue or be sued in tort. However, since infants lack capacity, any litigation must be conducted through an adult acting as guardian. It is through a guardian that infants may enforce their rights or have responsibilities enforced against them. Besides actions in tort, infants might use guardians to prevent the breach of a beneficial contract, to maintain property rights, or to protect an estate.

MARRIAGE BETWEEN INFANTS

State statutes provide a means by which infants may legally marry. Generally these statutes allow females to marry two or three years younger than their male counterparts. Some statutes require permission of a parent or legal guardian, while others do not. Some statutes allow males to marry two or three years before adulthood with permission of a parent or legal guardian, but most states require males to achieve adulthood.

If an infant should marry below the minimum statutory age, the marriage is voidable and subject to annulment. Should the infant marry within the minimum statutory age but without the requisite parental consent, the marriage usually is considered valid and not subject to annulment. Should the infant marry under the age of seven, the marriage absolutely is void under all circumstances.

Two problems may arise when only one of the parties to a marriage is an infant. If the infant is under the statutory age, the spouse may be guilty of contributing to the delinquency of a minor. It has been held that marriage to a female infant does not relieve the adult male of a potential statutory rape charge in the event he has had intercourse with the infant wife.

In addition to parental and guardian permission statutes, most states have provisions for infants under the age of parental consent to validly marry when the female is pregnant. Such marriages frequently are termed secret marriages, because the judge authorized to perform them may issue an order keeping the exact date of the marriage off the public record to protect the good name of the infant and her family.

When infant marriages take place, the law imposes upon the infant husband the duty of support and upon the infant wife the duty of care. These duties supersede prior existing duties to parents; and all rights of a husband and wife and a parent and child are attributed to the infant's new family unit. However, with respect to other provisions of the law, the infant marriage does not remove disabilities of infancy except as may be provided by statute.

INFANTS BORN OUT OF WEDLOCK

An infant born out of wedlock, who has also been conceived out of wedlock, is known as a bastard. The same is true of infants born of void marriages, and of infants born during wedlock but under such circumstances that make it impossible for the husband of the infant's mother to be the father. In the latter instance, it is absolutely necessary to show impossibility and not just separation. The law presumes legitimacy. Additionally, should the mother and father of the infant subsequently marry; should there be a recognition or acknowledgment by the father that the infant is his natural offspring; or if there should be a court decree declaring legitimacy, a bastard infant would be considered legitimate and would acquire all the rights of an infant born in lawful wedlock. In some states there are statutes which allow the infant to directly determine his or her paternity. When the infant is successful, it also is as if he or she was born in lawful wedlock.

While the duty for support of bastard infants at common law seemed to rest on no one, modern statutes have placed the burden on the mother when she has custody and control. As an alternative, most jurisdictions have passed statutes which allow for bastardy proceedings by the mother or the state against the putative father. When successful, these civil proceedings require the father to make support payments even though he may be an infant.

At common law a bastard was regarded as a nonperson and was not entitled to a name unless it was acquired through baptism or reputation. Under modern law, it is generally established that the infant has the right to the surname of the mother, not that of the father.

At common law a bastard had no rights of inheritance from the mother or the father, as inheritable blood was not considered to exist. Under modern law the infant has a right of inheritance from its mother, and from its father if the father acknowledges or recognizes the infant. Bastard infants generally do not inherit from each other or from legitimate offspring of the same mother. The estates of bastards go to their heirs and spouses but usually not to their natural parents.

The right of custody of a bastard infant rests with the natural parent, provided such parent is a fit and proper person and the welfare of the infant does not require state interference. Natural parent means both the father and mother, but the mother primarily has been considered the parent entitled to custody and control of the infant and entitled to receive the infant's services and earnings. Formerly the father was considered to have an interest only after that of the mother, and then only if he had a duty of support enforced against him. Today an unwed father may be considered a suitable parent along with the mother, whether or not a support order has been entered against him.

Infants who are born as a result of rape statutorily are legitimatized and have all the rights of legitimate children of their natural mother.

RIGHTS AND RESPONSIBILITIES BETWEEN PARENT AND INFANT

The relationship between a legitimate infant and its father or mother is both natural and legal: Natural in that it is the result of the union between husband and wife, and legal in that it is subject to the law of the state. Since common law, the state has had authority to break up family relationships where it can show that continuation is not in the best interest of the infant. However, the state does not intervene with any frequency, because in recognizing the natural right of parents to raise infants as they desire, state legislatures have statutorily limited the states' power of protection over the young.

At common law the natural father solely was responsible for his offspring and in exchange he received all the benefits from his offspring. Under modern law, fathers and mothers share responsibility and rewards. Thus, the rights of parents are considered to involve custody and control, a right to the infant's earnings and services, and obedience. The duties of parents are considered to involve support, education and protection. Rights and duties generally are looked upon as being reciprocal in that the parents have duties in exchange for their rights, and infants may expect to receive care, custody, protection and control from parents in return for the infants' obedience and contribution when called upon. The rights and duties last as long as an infant remains a minor. They may expire earlier if the infant becomes emancipated through marriage, military service or the parental renouncing of all legal rights and duties. However, an infant's rights and its parent's duties may extend into adulthood should the offspring suffer incapacity because of medical or physical disabilities. Many jurisdictions, but not all, have imposed this responsibility through legislation or common law interpretation. Legislation is required for an adult offspring to be liable for his or her sick or indigent parent, because such a duty was not recognized at common law. There are several state statutes of this nature, but all are concerned with adult offspring. Infants are not responsible for the support of their parents.

CUSTODY AND CARE

The custody and care of an infant by its parents generally has been interpreted to mean that the parents have a natural and legal right, against all other persons, to raise and care for the infant, so long as such custody and care is in the best interest of the child. The right, therefore, is not absolute nor is it a property right that can be bargained, sold or otherwise disposed of. In some jurisdictions, parents may agree between themselves to relinquish custody and care to one another, although concurrence by the local court normally is required in order to have the agreement binding on both parents, just as it is in divorce and separation cases. If one parent dies, a reasonably competent surviving parent has the right to custody and care of infants, even if the parents were divorced and the deceased parent had custody at the time of death. The same result prevails even where there had been an earlier abandonment by the living parent.

Custody further has been interpreted to include parental rights to their children's services or earnings. The thesis is that parental responsibility is compensated by the right to the services or their value. This right to services is looked upon as a property right devolving from the common law.

CONTROL

The control of an infant by its parents has been interpreted to include the right to make decisions concerning the infant's religious affiliations, place and kind of education, medical and dental treatment, and discipline. Control may also include protection and restriction of association with non-family members who, in the parents' judgment, are of unsatisfactory character; the parents' giving freely of advice without fear of libel and slander; and the right to name an infant. Control and custody, while often used interchangeably, are distinguishable in that control represents guidance of the infant while custody implies responsibility for the infant.

SUPPORT, MAINTENANCE AND EDUCATION

The parental duties of support, maintenance and education are moral as well as statutory. Unlike some changes from common law regarding rights, the father still is the legally responsible parent either until his death or until circumstances make it impossible for him to perform his duty. At that point the burden switches to the mother, if she is capable. A recent development in several jurisdictions indicates that a capable mother also is liable where a capable father fails to perform his obligations. Such a situation might arise where the father refuses to work, works but refuses to contribute, or just leaves the family. His obligation still exists, but the welfare of dependent infants would dictate that the mother must then support them. Where the mother does furnish support, courts in these jurisdictions likely would hold the father liable to her.

The father's obligation of support is not extinguished merely because infants have substantial independent estates which could properly maintain them at their station in life, or because infants are being supported by others, or because there is a legal separation between the parents and the mother has received custody of the infants, or because there is a separation without an award of custody. Aside from the father's death or incapacity, the only usual way his duty is avoided is through the infant's emancipation or adoption.

The minimum required support, maintenance and education for infants is dependent upon the parents' means, station in life and physical well being. Additionally, infants with independent income may not merit much beyond the basics of support from their parents, while by comparison the unhealthy and the poor may demand more.

Parental obligations are limited to those matters classified as necessities. That which is excessive is not a necessity, and the parent is not responsible even for goods and services purchased by others in the parents' name. Besides food, clothing and shelter, the following have been classified as necessities: education through college, legal expenses to defend or protect an infant, medical and dental care, and funeral expenses.

TORTS AND CONTRACTS

It generally is held that unemancipated infants may not be subjected to a suit in tort by their parents, nor may they sue their parents in tort. Infants have a right of action, through their guardian, against negligent or otherwise tortious third parties. Parents of these infants also have a right of action against negligent or otherwise tortious third parties, as the majority of jurisdictions allow parental suits on the basis of present or future loss of services and expenses due to injury. Some jurisdictions also allow parental suits against third persons for mental anxiety and loss of their children's affection.

Contractual obligations of infants are voidable when made with parents just as they are when made with third parties. Parental contracts with adult offspring are not voidable ipso facto, but because of the possibility of undue influence or even fraud they will be scrutinized more closely if largely advantageous to one of the parties. This same close scrutiny also is exercised in situations involving gifts.

ADOPTIVE AND LOCO PARENTIS PARENTS

Adoptive parents and parents in loco parentis are treated in law the same as natural parents. They are entitled to custody and control of the infant, to the services and earnings of the infant, and to tort recovery for the loss of those services. In return the adoptive and in loco parentis parents have the duties to guide, protect, educate, support and maintain the infant. One becomes an adoptive parent only through court order. One becomes a parent in loco parentis through voluntary assumption of the status and obligations of a parent without adoption. Thus a parent in loco parentis might be a stepparent, a foster parent, a grandparent or a friend; but one is not a parent in loco parentis by this relationship without assuming the status and obligations of a parent.

SCHOOLING, RIGHTS AND RESPONSIBILITIES

It is the duty of parents to educate their infants. This duty has been placed upon parents because they are the natural parties to teach. They generally do most, if not all, teaching for the first five years of an infant's life, at which time they are assisted by a public or private formal school system. It is the formal school system and its relationship to the parent and infant that is covered under this topic.

The free public school privilege available to infants is a constitutional right and a duty imposed upon them for the public good. It is required of all infants except those who are disruptive to the school system, those who have successfully completed their academic work, those who have achieved a certain age in relation to their academic standing, and those for whom the school system does not have the necessary facilities. Thus, under normal circumstances, all infants have free education available to them. This even includes indigents who would be fed and clothed by the school board in order that they might partake of the opportunity for education.

Many of the problems associated with families and schools have arisen over school rules and regulations promulgated by the state, school boards, school administrators and teachers. The basic tenor of the court decisions is that rules and regulations cannot be contrary to federal and state constitutions and legislation, and they must be reasonable in substance and enforcement. Thus, racial segregation through separate but equal schools has been held invalid; extension or reduction of the school year or changing of textbooks contrary to statute has been held invalid; and, unreasonable regulations concerning hairstyles, off campus activities, flag saluting and underground newspapers have been held invalid. However, residency requirements, health regulations including statutory vaccination requirements, school placements, and reasonable rules and regulations for hairstyles, off campus activities, underground and school papers, demonstrations, smoking, and secret societies have been held to be valid. In resolving such issues courts must determine whether the constitution or other legislation is applicable, and if it is, whether the school has complied. If the constitution or other legislation is not applicable, the courts must then determine the reasonableness of a rule in relation to the school's being able to effectively manage itself.

Inasmuch as school management requires rules and regulations, and since even reasonable rules and regulations are broken, the school has been authorized to serve in loco parentis for the purposes of discipline, control and punishment of children. The teacher, administration, school board, and state are required to exercise such powers of control, discipline and punishment as are necessary and reasonable to manage schools effectively. In this respect, courts have ruled that such discipline as permanent exclusion, temporary expulsion, and suspension are proper if they are exercised by an appropriate official, on proper grounds, and in compliance with due process requirements.

Due process does not require the extensive due process procedures of criminal proceedings, but it does require the fundamental basics of a student's being advised of the substance of the infraction and given the opportunity to prepare a defense, to present mitigating circumstances, and have the identity of principal witnesses disclosed. Another form of discipline used principally in the lower grades, involves reasonable corporal punishment by teachers or school administrators. The punishment is not reasonable when exercised in a wanton, malicious or extravagant manner, and such punishment must be fitting the seriousness of the offense.

Other aspects of school management rights concerning parents and children have to do with grading, promotion, demotion, classes, class size, curriculum and textbooks. Where there is neither legislation nor a school system directive, the classroom teacher will be responsible. However, in most instances teacher prerogatives are limited to grading, homework, text selection and possibly choice of curriculum. The teacher's exercise of his or her prerogative is governed by reasonableness, except possibly with regard to homework. Some cases have approved homework assignments even when they are unreasonably burdensome for the student.

Textbooks are to be furnished free, and curriculum choices, when available, may be selected by the parents. Graduation is the culmination of the educational experience and can not be denied by the school authorities to those who have completed the prescribed courses with appropriate scholarship.

Federal and state programs to assist public, private and parochial schools have been established under the National School Lunch Act, the Child Nutrition Act and State School Transportation Acts. In order for a school to qualify under the Federal Acts, the lunch or breakfast program must be nonprofit and must cover needy children. Free transportation is considered part of a free school system because of the compulsory attendance laws. Thus, free transportation must be available to all students who live the requisite distance from their schools, whether they are attending a public, private or parochial school.

PARENTS' LIABILITY FOR ACTS OF INFANTS

Under common law the parental relationship by itself did not make parents liable for the torts or crimes of their children. Today, there are a few exceptions to this general rule that carries over from common law. A parent may be liable in tort where the parent is the principal and the infant acted as an agent; where the parent failed to exercise control over the infant when it was known, or through the exercise of due care it should have been known, that injury to another would be a natural consequence of the failure to control; or where there has been entrustment of a dangerous instrument such as a gun to an infant unfamiliar with firearms operation, or the entrustment of an automobile to an incapable driver. Under some state and municipal statutes there also is imposed a civil responsibility for parents to financially reimburse, usually in a limited amount, the victims of their infants' malicious or wilful destruction of property. And, of course, parents would be liable individually if they were parties to a tort or crime committed by their infants.

8

The American View On Awarding Attorney's Fees— The Alaskan Pipeline Cases

Barry Lee Myers*

When a major oil field was discovered on the North Slope of Alaska in 1968, it could not have been anticipated that the event would lead to a major pronouncement by the United States Supreme Court in 1975 on the award- ing of attorney's fees to successful litigants in civil suits. Nevertheless, the seven year chronology of events resulted in a definitive statement of the appli- cability of the so called American Rule regarding attorney's fees awards in civil litigation in which the plaintiff's position equates with a significant public interest.

Questions pertaining to attorney's fees as a cost element in litigation and as a possible component of a damage award are frequently raised by students in introductory law courses. Such questions are often just answered by the generalized response that in American courts each party pays his or her own legal fees. But there are significant policy issues involved in the question of whether certain parties should be awarded attorney's fees. Having to pay lawyer's fees raises the cost of litigation. A policy which might shift those fees to the losing party could have significant impact upon the willingness of parties to litigate a case. This issue will be explored in this chapter by looking at the historic and contemporary treatment of the problem. The entire issue will be placed against the backdrop of the very interesting situation surround- ing the construction of the Alaskan pipeline.

HISTORICAL DEVELOPMENT

The American Rule is the label given the legal proposition generally fol- lowed by American courts in rejecting claims by winning litigants for com-

*The Pennsylvania State University

pensation to defray the expenditure they have made to pay their lawyer. The rule is called "American" because it differs from the English approach which, as a general rule, upholds the opposite viewpoint.

The contemporary English practice evolved from the Statute of Gloucester, enacted in 1275. That statute enabled certain plaintiffs to recover their court costs which the courts interpreted to include lawyer's fees. In 1607, winning defendants were statutorily accorded similar rights. The contemporary English practice is that successful litigating parties are routinely awarded attorney's fees. Most of the advanced nations take a similar approach to the awarding of attorney's fees.

In light of this historic background, it might be asked what led to a contrary position by American courts. Several theories have been advanced by legal commentators, but no single explanation seems sufficient. Some assert that the change resulted from historical accident as some early attorney's fees statutes fell into disuse through inadvertence or through failure of fee schedules imposed by some statutes to keep pace with the actual cost of litigation. Others believe the no fee rule arose from the distrust of lawyers which existed in the seventeenth century. Whatever the reason for the divergence of American jurisprudence on this point, a reason which is partially obscured by the sands of time, American courts do adhere to the general principle that lawyer's fees are borne by the respective parties to a suit and are not taxable to the loser.

EFFECT OF ATTORNEY'S FEES ON LITIGATION

Aside from stating the difference between the English and American rules it is worthwhile to explore the effect that the two rules have upon litigation and access to the courts. However, because no objective comparative study exists, the rules can be evaluated only subjectively by exploring the theorized impact and then applying one's value system to characterize the impact as either desirable or undesirable.

It can be argued that failure to award attorney's fees to a victorious party discourages the free exercise of one's rights to a judicial determination because the cost of counsel deters the initiation, defense or continuing prosecution of a lawsuit. This argument is especially persuasive in cases where a litigating party seeks injunctive relief rather than damages. With equal force the opposing point can be argued. That is, since lawsuits generally involve honest disputes, the losing party should not be assessed his opponent's lawyer's fees. Taxing those fees to the loser increases the possible loss on judgment and thereby discourages the aggressive defense of lawsuits. Instead, cases may be settled to insure that large sums will not have to be paid.

EXCEPTIONS TO THE RULE

The American Rule is not absolute. Specific statutory exceptions have been created by state legislatures and Congress. The states of Alaska, Nevada and

Oregon have enacted sweeping exceptions which make the American rule the exception rather than the rule. At the federal level the Clayton Antitrust Act, the Securities Act of 1933, the Truth-in-Lending Act, the Fair Labor Standards Act, the federal water and air pollution acts, the Ocean Dumping Act, the Civil Rights Act of 1964, and numerous other federal statutes, about fifty in all, provide for the award of attorney's fees at the discretion of the courts. However, it is not clear what reasons underlie the decision of Congress to provide fee shifting in these instances but not in others. Some statutes provide fee shifting only in favor of successful plaintiffs while others allow recovery by either winning party; some statutes allow recovery only between private ligigants while others allow recovery against the government when it is a losing party.

Besides these statutory exceptions to the American Rule, certain court fashioned exceptions exist as well. Equity courts, retaining the original power of the chancellor to do equity in a given case, can and do on occasion award attorney's fees. These instances of judicial exception to the general rule occur in two basic situations: first, in those cases where the prevailing party should not have had to litigate to secure his or her rights but was forced to do so by the unjustified intransigence of the losing party; and, second, where the winning party has served some broad public interest or secured some public right which the public at large was entitled to. This second instance is called the "private attorney general" situation. The label of "private attorney general" arises because the private person acting to secure the public right is acting as though he had the position of an attorney general whose function is to protect the public interest.

The exercise of judicial authority in awarding attorney's fees to private attorneys general expanded significantly during the 1970's, particularly in the federal courts. The lower federal courts awarded fees in cases involving consumer groups, civil rights groups, and environmental groups when they were litigating public interest questions. The allowance of attorney fee recovery in these cases defrayed the largest expense these public interest groups faced in pursuing injunctive and declaratory relief against large corporate organizations and the government. The controversy generated by the North Slope oil discovery was destined to bring the issue of these expanding exceptions to the American Rule to the U.S. Supreme Court.

THE ALASKAN PIPELINE CASES

Following the 1968 oil find, it was quickly realized that the location of the oil reservoir at Prudhoe Bay on the North Slope was a climatologically unsuitable spot from which to ship the oil from Alaska. Accordingly, one of the most challenging private engineering projects of modern times would be undertaken—a 48 inch diameter pipeline would be built from Prudhoe Bay to the Port of Valdez located on the southern coast of Alaska. The pipeline would be 789 miles long and would traverse some of the most forbidding terrain on the North American continent. A group of major oil companies—Atlantic Richfield, Humble and British Petroleum—formed the Trans-Alaska Pipeline System in 1968 to undertake the project. Approximately 95 percent of all land in the State of Alaska is owned by the federal government. As a result, the pipeline route would traverse 641 miles of lands owned by the United States. The pipeline company would need permission to cross this land. In June 1969, it made application to the Department of Interior for the needed right-of-way permits.

By that time a great deal of concern had developed over the possible environmental damage that could occur from the construction and operation of the pipeline. The Wilderness Society, the Environmental Defense Funds, Inc., and Friends of the Earth, three environmental interest groups, brought suit in federal district court requesting an injunction against the Secretary of the Interior to prevent issuance of the needed right-of-way permits. The environmental groups sought the injunction on two grounds. First, permits of the type sought by the pipeline company could be issued under the Mineral Leasing Act of 1920, but that statute only allowed rights-of-way to be of a maximum width equal to the pipeline plus twenty-five feet on each side—54 feet for the pipeline, its construction and operation. Construction of the line required more space as would certain aspects of its later operation. Thus, it was questionable whether the Mineral Leasing Act could serve as the basis for the type of permit required. Second, no Environmental Impact Statement (EIS) had been prepared as required by the then newly enacted National Environmental Policy Act. Accordingly, the court issued a preliminary injunction against the issuance of the permits.

In 1970, the Trans-Alaska Pipeline System was replaced by the Alyeska Pipeline Service Company (Alyeska). Alyeska was a broader based company than its predecessor; its stock was owned by ARCO Pipeline Company, Sohio Pipeline Company, Humble Pipeline Company, Mobil Pipeline Company, Phillips Petroleum Company, Armerada Hess Corporation, and Union Oil Company of California.

Between 1970 and 1972 the Interior Department prepared the required EIS and agreed with Alyeska to get around the right-of-way width limitation by issuing special land use permits (SLUPs) instead of actual right-of-way grants. On August 15, 1972, the district court dissolved its preliminary injunction of two years prior. The Wilderness Society and the other environmental groups appealed the dissolution decision of the U.S. Court of Appeals. On February 9, 1973, that court reversed the district court and reinstated the injunction holding that the SLUPs could not be used to circumvent the narrow right-of-way allowed by the Mineral Leasing Act of 1920. Because the pipeline could not be built without the right-of-way permits, the Court of Appeals did not address the question of whether the prepared EIS was adequate, leaving that question for later determination if it became necessary. On April 2, 1973, the U.S. Supreme Court refused the petition for a writ of certiorari thereby letting the Court of Appeals decision stand. The Wilderness Society had stopped the pipeline. It had won the judicial battle, but would soon lose the environmental war.

On November 16, 1973, at the time of the oil crisis, the Trans-Alaska Pipeline Authorization Act was signed into law. The act was a specific reaction to the injunction issued in February of that year. The Pipeline Act removed the basis for the injunction by amending the Mineral Leasing Act of 1920 to provide for the needed rights-of-way. It bypassed the National Environmental Policy Act by accepting the already drafted EIS as satisfactory. It provided for preferential judicial review of any further issues which might arise in connection with the project. And, it specifically divested the U.S. Court of Appeals of any right to review future pipeline cases by requiring that appeals be taken directly to the Supreme Court. The pipeline would be built.

Prior to the November 16th Act, the Wilderness Society and the other environmental groups had petitioned the federal court requesting that it exercise its equitable powers under the private attorney general concept and award to them a judgment against the Department of Interior and Alyeska for the reasonable cost of their attorney's fees—which ran in the hundreds of thousands of dollars. The appeals court upheld the private attorney general exception to the American Rule in the opinion below. The Supreme Court took the case on appeal. The Supreme Court opinion follows immediately that of the U.S. Court of Appeals.

■ ■ ■

WILDERNESS SOCIETY v. MORTON
United States Court of Appeals, District of Columbia
495 F.2d 1028 (1974)

J. Skelly Wright, Circuit Judge: Appellants Wilderness Society, Environmental Defense Funds, Inc. and Friends of the Earth request an award of expenses and attorneys' fees related to the litigation they successfully prosecuted to bar construction of the trans-Alaska pipeline. * * * With respect to the main issue posed, we hold that an award of attorneys' fees is appropriate and remand the case to the District Court to determine the fees.

There have always existed equitable exceptions to the traditional American rule barring recovery of attorneys' fees by a successful litigant. In cases in which a party has acted in bad faith, assessment of fees properly serves to punish that party's obdurate behavior. Another exception includes cases in which the plaintiff's suit confers a benefit on the members of an ascertainable class and in which an award of fees will serve to spread the costs of litigation among its beneficiaries.

Neither of these historic exceptions is applicable here. Appellees' legal position as to the meaning of the Mineral Leasing Act and relevant administrative regulations, though ultimately rejected by the court, was manifestly reasonable and assumed in good faith. . . * * *

The Supreme Court has recently indicated, however, that the equitable power of federal courts to award attorneys' fees when the interests of justice so require is not a narrow power confined to rigid sets of cases. Rather, it "is part of the original authority of the chancellor to do equity in a particular situation," and should be used whenever "overriding considerations indicate the need for such a recovery."

Recognizing their broad equitable power, some courts have concluded that the interests of justice require fee shifting in a third class of cases where the plaintiff acted as a "'private attorney general,' vindicating a policy that Congress considered of the highest priority." * * *

* * * It is a paramount principle of equity that the court will go much farther both to grant and to withhold relief in furtherance of the public interest than when only private interests are involved. * * *

* * * Where the law relies on private suits to effectuate congressional policy in favor of broad public interests, attorneys' fees are often necessary to ensure that private litigants will initiate such suits. Substantial benefits to the general

public should not depend upon the financial status of the individual volunteering to serve as plaintiff or upon the charity of public-minded lawyers. * * *

The chief rationale behind the American rule is the notion that parties might be unjustly discouraged from instituting or defending actions to vindicate their rights if the penalty for losing in court included the fees of their opponent's counsel. * * *

Whatever force this argument concededly has in the great run of civil litigation, we think it plainly inapposite to the circumstances of the present case. As Alyeska has so often brought to our attention, the value of its investment at stake in this litigation was over a billion dollars. Each week's delay in constructing the pipeline imposed an additional $3.5 million in costs. An award of fees in this case, though conceivably large in absolute sense, will be paltry in comparison with the interest Alyeska had in defending this appeal. Where the interest at stake is many times greater than the expected cost of one's opponent's attorney's fees, any possibility of deterrence is surely remote if not nonexistent. * * *

Looking at this case from appellants' point of view, the unavailability of attorneys' fees might significantly deter them from having brought this meritorious litigation. In prosecuting this case, appellants undertook litigation of monumental proportions. According to their bill of costs, the matters appealed consumed over 4,500 hours of lawyers' time, all in addition to the efforts before the District Court in 1970 when this action was commenced and preliminary relief obtained. This burden was assumed not in the hope of obtaining a monetary award, nor to protect an interest peculiar to appellants and their members, but rather to vindicate important statutory rights of all citizens whose interests might be affected by construction of the pipeline. * * *

* * * In the final analysis, this case involved the duty of the Executive Branch to observe the restrictions imposed by the Legislative, and the primary responsibility of the Congress under the Constitution to regulate the use of public lands. * * *

In sum, the equities of this particular case support an award of attorneys' fees to the successful plaintiff-appellants. Acting as private attorneys general, not only have they ensured the proper functioning of our system of government, but they have advanced and protected in a very concrete manner substantial public interests. An award of fees would not have unjustly discouraged appellee Alyeska from defending its case in court. And denying fees might well have deterred appellants from undertaking the heavy burden of this litigation.

Even if fees are to be awarded under a private attorney general theory, a question is posed as to whether Alyeska should bear them. Technically, it is the Interior Department, on Alyeska's application, which violated the Mineral Leasing Act by granting rights-of-way in excess of the Act's width restrictions, and it is the Interior Department's failure to comply with NEPA which was challenged on appeal. [H]owever, no attorneys' fees can be imposed against the United States. Alyeska argues that it is inappropriate to circumvent the statute by taxing it for a dereliction not its own.

Fee shifting under the private attorney general theory, however, is not intended to punish law violators, but rather to ensure that those who have acted to protect the public interest will not be forced to shoulder the entire cost of litigation. After successfully persuading the Interior Department to grant the rights-of-way, Alyeska intervened in this litigation to protect its massive interests. Since Alyeska unquestionably was a major and a real party at interest in this case, actively participating in the litigation along with the Government, we think it fair that it should bear part of the attorneys' fees. In recognition of the Government's role in the case, on the other hand, Alyeska should have to bear only half of the total fees. The other half is properly allocated to the Government and, because of the statutory bar, must be assumed by appellants. In this manner the equitable principle that appellees bear their fair share of this litigation's full cost and the congressional policy that the United States not be taxable for fees can be accommodated. * * *

An order will enter awarding statutory costs, and the bill of costs is remanded to the District Court for the setting of attorneys' fees.

So ordered.

Wilkey, Circuit Judge, joined by MacKinnon and Robb, Circuit Judges, dissenting.

We respectfully dissent. It is difficult to see that either of these plaintiffs "acted as a "private attorney general, vindicating a policy that Congress considered of the highest priority." Judging from Congress' most recent action, these plaintiffs have been frustrating the policy Congress considers highly desirable and of the utmost urgency.

Nor do we agree that "this litigation may well have provided substantial benefits to particular individuals." Aside from the numerous lawyers involved, we are at a loss to know who those "particular individuals" enjoying "substantial benefits" might be. It is hard to visualize the average American in this winter of 1973-74, turning down his thermostat and with a careful eye on his auto fuel gauge, feeling that warm glow of gratitude to those public-spirited plaintiffs in the Alaska Pipeline case. * * *

This stands as plaintiffs' net achievement: the amendment of the 1920 Mineral Leasing Act to authorize a wider right of way, quite the opposite of the plaintiffs' objective to limit the right of way to 25 feet on each side. Against this public service must be weighed the public disservice in blocking access to the much needed oil at a critical time in our history, and the enormously higher cost we must all pay. As the majority states (p. 1032): "Each week's delay in constructing the pipeline imposed an additional $3.5 million in costs." This is $182 million per year. Plaintiffs' litigation has lasted over three and a half years, the delay is at least as long as the litigation, so construction costs have been upped at least $637 million—well over half a billion dollars, all of which will be paid for by the American consumer, when the oil finally arrives. ■ ■ ■

■ ■ ■

ALYESKA PIPELINE SERVICE COMPANY v.
THE WILDERNESS SOCIETY
United States Supreme Court
95 S. Ct. 1613 (1975)

Mr. Justice White delivered the opinion of the Court.

* * * The Court of Appeals awarded attorneys' fees to respondents against petitioner Alyeska Pipeline Service Co. based upon the Court's equitable powers and the theory that respondents were entitled to fees because they were performing the services of a "private attorney general." Certiorari was granted to determine whether this award of attorneys' fees was appropriate. We reverse. * * *

* * * Since there was no applicable statutory authorization for such an award, the [C]ourt [of Appeals] proceeded to consider whether the requested fee award fell within any of the exceptions to the general "American rule" that the prevailing party may not recover attorneys' fees as costs or otherwise. * * *

In the United States, the prevailing litigant is ordinarily not entitled to collect a reasonable attorneys' fee from the loser. We are asked to fashion a far-reaching exception to this "American Rule"; but having considered its origin and development, we are convinced that it would be inappropriate for the Judiciary, without legislative guidance, to reallocate the burdens of litigation in the manner and to the extent urged by respondents and approved by the Court of Appeals.

At common law, costs were not allowed; but for centuries in England there has been statutory authorization to award costs, including attorneys' fees. Although the matter is in the discretion of the court, counsel fees are regularly allowed to the prevailing party.

During the first years of the federal court system, Congress provided through legislation that the federal courts were to follow the practice with respect to awarding attorneys' fees of the courts of the States in which the federal courts were located, with the exception of district courts under admiralty and maritime jurisdiction which were to follow a specific fee schedule. Those statutes, by 1800, had either expired or been repealed.

In 1796, this Court appears to have ruled that the Judiciary would not itself create a general rule, independent of any statute, allowing awards of attorneys' fees in federal courts. * * *

The practice after 1799 and until 1853 continued as before, that is, with the federal courts referring to the state rules governing awards of counsel fees, although the express legislative authorization for that practice had expired. By legislation in 1842, Congress did give this Court authority to prescribe the items and amounts of costs which could be taxed in federal courts but the Court took no action under this statutory mandate.

In 1853, Congress undertook to standardize the costs allowable in federal litigation. In support of the proposed legislation, it was asserted that there was great diversity in practice among the courts and that losing litigants were being unfairly saddled with exorbitant fees for the victor's attorney. The result was a far-reaching act specifying in detail the nature and amount of the taxable items of cost in the federal courts. One of its purposes was to limit allowances for attorneys' fees that were to be charged to the losing parties. * * *

* * * The 1853 Act was carried forward in the Revised Statutes of 1874 and by the Judicial Code of 1911. Its substance, without any apparent intent to change the controlling rules, was also included in the revised code of 1948 as §§ 1920 and 1923(a). Under § 1920, a court may tax as costs the various items specified, including the "docket fees" under § 1923(a). That section provides that "[a]ttorney's and proctor's docket fees in courts of the United States may be taxed as costs as follows. . ." Against this background, this Court understandably declared in 1967 that with the exception of the small amounts allowed by § 1923, the rule "has long been that attorney's fees are not ordinarly recoverable. . ."

To be sure, the fee statutes have been construed to allow, in limited circumstances, a reasonable attorneys' fee to the prevailing party in excess of the small sums permitted by § 1923. [T]he 1853 Act was read as not interfering with the historic power of equity. . .

Congress has not repudiated the judicially fashioned exceptions to the general rule against allowing substantial attorney fees; but neither has it retracted, repealed or modified the limitations on taxable fees contained in the 1853 statute and its successors. Nor has it extended any roving authority to the Judiciary to allow counsel fees as costs or otherwise whenever the courts might deem them warranted. What Congress has done, however, while fully recognizing and accepting the general rule, is itself to make specific and explicit provisions for the allowance of attorneys' fees under selected statues granting or protecting various federal rights. These statutory allowances are now available in a variety of circumstances, but they also differ considerably among themselves. * * *

It is true that under some, if not most, of the statutes providing for the allowance of reasonable fees, Congress has opted to rely heavily on private enforcement to implement public policy and to allow counsel fees so as to encourage private litigation. * * * But congressional utilization of the private attorney general concept can in no sense be construed as a grant of authority to the Judiciary to jettison the traditional rule against nonstatutory allowances to the prevailing party and to award attorneys' fees whenever the courts deem the public policy furthered by a particular statute important enough to warrant the award. * * *

We need labor the matter no further. It appears to us that the rule suggested here and adopted by the Court of Appeals would make major inroads on a policy matter that Congress has reserved for itself. Since the approach taken by Congress to this issue has been to carve out specific exceptions to a general rule that federal courts cannot award attorneys' fees . . . those courts are not free to fashion drastic new rules with respect to the allowance of attorneys' fees to the prevailing party in federal litigation or to pick and choose among plaintiffs and the statutes under which they sue and to award fees in some cases but not in others, depending upon the courts' assessment of the importance of the public policies involved in particular cases. Nor should the federal courts purport to adopt on their own initiative a rule awarding attorneys' fees based on the private attorney general approach when such judicial rule will operate only against private parties and not against the Government.

We do not purport to assess the merits or demerits of the "American rule" with respect to the allowance of attorneys' fees. It has been criticized in recent years, and courts have been urged to find exceptions to it. It is also apparent from our national experience that the encouragement of private action to implement public policy has been viewed as desirable in a variety of circumstances. But the rule followed in our courts with respect to attorneys' fees has survived. It is deeply rooted in our history and in congressional policy; and it is not for us to invade the legislature's province by redistributing litigation costs in the manner suggested by respondents and followed by the Court of Appeals.

The decision below must therefore be reversed.

So ordered.

Reversed.

■ ■ ■

SELECTED BIBLIOGRAPHY

Ceder, Philip M., *Defrosting the Alyeska Chill: The Future of Attorneys' Fee Awards in Environmental Litigation.* 5 **Environmental Affairs** 297 (1976).

Miller, Terry M., *The Discretionary Award of Attorney's Fees by the Federal Courts: Selective Deviation from the No-Fee Rule and the Regrettably Brief Life of the Private Attorney General Doctrine.,* 36 **Ohio State Law Journal** 589 (1975).

Sands, C. Dallas, *Attorney's Fees as Recoverable Costs,* 63 **American Bar Association Journal** 510 (April 1977).

9

A Legal - Economic Dichotomy: Contribution To Failure in Regulatory Policy

Bartley A. Brennan*

It seems to me that every lawyer ought to seek an understanding of economics. The present divorce between the schools of political economy and the law seems to me an evidence of how much progress in philosophical study still remains to be made. Holmes, *The Path of the Law* (1896).

Mr. Justice Holmes' comment as to the need for a cross-fertilization of economics and law is important today in light of apparent failures in federal regulatory policy. Lawyers and economists predominate in policymaking roles within regulatory agencies and executive branch departments, yet they fail to communicate well at a theoretical level. This failure has led over a period of years to the development of conflicting objectives for governmental regulation of business, particularly in the area of antitrust law.

This chapter explores the difference in models which law and economics use as a guide to regulation of private entities. The failure of the legal model operating independently without consideration of key economic variables is illustrated in a brief examination of antitrust laws as applied to the cement industry. The chapter concludes with an evaluation of the contribution of law and economics to regulatory policy in the antitrust area.

THE DICHOTOMY OF LEGAL AND ECONOMIC THINKING IN REGULATORY POLICY

The theoretical models which form the framework for legal and economic analysis of government regulation involve conflicting perceptions as to when courts and government agencies should regulate private entities and as to

*Bowling Green State University

what standards should be used in such efforts. For one trained in the law the adversarial model represents the best avenue to attain both private and public goals. Regulation is perceived as a conflict between those charged with protecting the public and business entities operating for profit, the latter seeking unrestrained assess to the marketplace in order to pursue what they see as legitimate economic activity. Following argumentation between the staff of a regulatory body and counsel representing the private entity, an independent board of commissioners or a single administrator attempts to arrive at a decision which best serves the public. The economist, on the other hand, sees regulation as a substitute for the factors of supply and demand, which when operating through the price mechanism, normally distributes resources in the most efficient manner. It is the absence of the normal workings of the price mechanism which justifies regulation, particularly in such basic industries as the telephone, telegraph, and other utilities. Duplication of utility services is considered by the economist as a misallocation of resources. Thus, the emphasis for the legal model is on the *control* of *conduct* of private entities which is adjudged in individual cases to lessen actual or potential competition. For the economist regulation has as its goal the *control* of the *market* and the efficient use of resources. If the two models based on different assumptions and objectives continue merely to co-exist within the same agency structure, law trained decision makers will continue to make judgments based on data coming from economic models whose assumptions, structure, and predictive objectives they often misunderstand or ignore.

Professor Edward Mason early recognized this conflict between the disciplines as to structure and goals for regulation. He noted for instance that the term "monopoly" (and its antithesis "competition") is used in the law as a standard of evaluation, not as a tool of analysis as in economics.[1] Under a legal approach, government regulation of private entities is directed toward the development of a public policy which concerns itself with the evaluation of specific business conduct such as price fixing or territorial restrictions (where manufacturers limit the geographical area in which a retailer or jobber can sell). Courts and government agencies first attempt to distinguish between business practices which serve the public interest and business practices which do not. They classify these practices either as competitive and in the public interest or monopolistic, and if unregulated, contrary to public policy. Their conclusions are based on the use of tests outlined by the courts in previous cases, or by statutory standards set out by the Congress or state legislatures. An example might be a court's consideration of whether a certain form of business conduct is "reasonable." A defendant accused of predatory conduct and violating the antitrust laws attempts to show that because its conduct is similar to that which the court or agency held to be "reasonable" in a previous case, that case should be binding in the present litigation.

Economists, on the other hand, have drawn away from the task of evaluation and prescription and moved toward mathematical model building. They seek to analyze each factual situation from a perspective of how resources will be most efficiently allocated. Traditionally, economists have believed that resource allocation will take place most efficiently when the law encourages the operating of forces of supply and demand to bring about an equilibrium price level for a particular product in a given market. This analytical orientation has led many economists dealing with industrial organization problems to recognize that monopoly elements exist in the practices of a large number of firms in all markets. These economists believe that we should accept the fact that pure or perfect competition in a highly industrialized society is an unrealistic and sometimes undesirable goal (in terms of optimal allocation of resources). They believe that we should concentrate on constructing an analytical model whose assumptions are more realistic in an era of oligopolistic markets. Present regulatory models constructed for the purpose of retaining markets where vigorous competition between many sellers and many buyers takes place may not serve the public interest or provide an optimal allocation of resources.

The basic gap between law and economics as to goals and models for regulation of private entities persists. As Justice Holmes and Professor Mason warned, neither the legal nor the economic approach operating independently is a sound basis for policy forumulation. This becomes evident when one examines the results of government antitrust regulation in the cement industry. The bias of the legal model and the unwillingness of law trained decision makers to incorporate significant economic variables in attempting to regulate a basic industry are illustrated in the following pages.

AN ILLUSTRATION OF THE DICHOTOMY OF LEGAL AND ECONOMIC THOUGHT IN ANTITRUST REGULATION

BACKGROUND

Faced with the prospect of increasing excess capacity and declining prices in the late 1950's, a number of cement producers attempted to improve their economic situation through selective acquisitions of large ready-mix concrete producers. Some 34 mergers took place between 1950 and 1967. Alarmed and concerned, Congress ordered the Federal Trade Commission (Commission) to prepare a study and offer some policy recommendations as to what measures should be taken to halt this trend. The economic research staff of the Commission prepared a study (Staff Report) which concluded that the merger of any of the large concrete makers with a substantial number of cement suppliers in a local market could adversely effect all firms in such a market.[2] The study was released in April, 1966 and an enforcement policy was set forth in January, 1967. What follows is an analysis of two leading decisions in which the Federal Trade Commission and two federal courts of appeal refused to allow cement producers to retain previously acquired ready-mix concrete plants. A brief summary of the cases precedes the analysis.

SUMMARY OF FACTS AND DECISIONS

In *Mississippi River Corporation* v. *F.T.C.* the defendant, Mississippi, acquired three companies engaged in the production of ready-mix concrete which were the largest purchasers of cement in Kansas City, Missouri, Memphis, Tennessee and Cincinnati, Ohio. Following these acquisitions Mississipi built a cement manufacturing company in St. Louis which would provide the needed cement for its acquired concrete companies in their geographical markets. On January 22, 1965, the Federal Trade Commission's staff issued a complaint charging Mississippi with a violation of Section 7 of the Clayton Act in that its acquisition of the three concrete companies would substantially lessen competition in the cement markets of Kansas City, Memphis and Cincinnati. It was alleged that Mississippi would usurp that portion of the cement market which suppliers of the three previously independent concrete companies had competed for. At the initial stage of litigation, the Hearing Examiner (examiner) ruled in favor of Mississippi and dismissed the complaint. On appeal by the FTC staff, the full Commission reversed the examiner and ordered Mississippi to divest itself of the acquired concrete companies. The United States Court of Appeals in 1972 affirmed the Commission's ruling.[3]

In *United States Steel Corporation* v. *FTC* the defendant, U.S. Steel, through its Atlas Cement Division, acquired in 1964 Certified Industries, a ready-mix concrete producer and the largest customer for all suppliers of cement in the New York City area. U.S. Steel is one of the nation's largest cement manufacturers and is the largest in the New York City area with particularly heavy production in three adjacent states. On January 22, 1965, the Federal Trade Commission's staff issued a complaint alleging a violation of Section 7 of the Clayton Act in that this acquisition would substantially lessen competition in the New York City cement market. The Hearing Examiner issued a decision dismissing the complaint against U.S. Steel, and the Commission on appeal reversed the examiner and ruled against U.S. Steel ordering its divestiture of Certified Industries. On May 6, 1970 the United States Court of Appeals affirmed this ruling.[4]

In both cases, the reversal of the hearing examiner reveals a bias of the Commission and the courts of appeal toward evaluating mergers by using traditional legal criteria of conduct and structure while ignoring economic variables considered important by the examiners and outlined by the Economic Research Bureau of the Commission in the *Staff Report*. The Report analyzed the cement industry using a concept of "workable competition." For economists this term has come to mean that mergers are not to be judged solely on pure or perfect competition criteria. Courts, in the economists view, should not judge mergers as harmful to the market based solely on the acquiring firm's present or potential conduct. Instead, they should use a range of criteria inclusive of: conduct of the firm and structure of the market, as well as the acquiring firm's performance following the merger. Overall industry performance should also be considered in a merger decision. The assumption underlying the workable competition concept is that the pure/perfect competition standard is both an unrealistic and undesirable policy objective in light of the fact that most basic industries (such as cement) possess a structure which provides for the intermingling of competitive and monopolistic elements. What follows is an analysis of how each criterion included in the term "workable competition" was viewed in the previously noted cases.

ANALYSIS OF CEMENT INDUSTRY LITIGATION USING WORKABLE COMPETITION CRITERIA

CONDUCT CRITERIA:

Such factors as predatory behavior toward present competitors, foreclosure of potential entrants into a market, price discrimination and the improper use of trade associations are indications of "bad conduct" under the Sherman and Clayton Act. Section 7 of the Clayton Act forbids the acquisitions of assets of a corporation the effect of which may be to substantially lessen competition or tend to create a monopoly. Using these basic statutes, the FTC *Staff Report* on the cement industry concluded that acquisition by cement producers of ready-mix concrete plants was a method of foreclosing potential rivals and obtaining captive purchasers of cement. The *Report* concluded on the basis of its examination of acquisitions from 1955-1965 that the major motivation of cement producers for acquiring concrete plants was to secure market outlets for their cement and thus to drive out competitors who did not own concrete plants. It noted that the high capital requirements barrier for entrance into the cement industry prevented any new competitors except for firms already established in other lines of activity such as fuel suppliers and ready mix concrete producers.

In the *Mississippi* and *U.S. Steel* cases, the initial decisions of the examiners were based upon the conduct criteria used in the *Staff Report*. Both decisions were based on a finding that there was more vigorous competition between major rivals in the relevant markets following the acquisitions. Evidence introduced on behalf of both cement firms showed that there were no potential entrants into the cement markets in Memphis, St. Louis, Cincinnati and New York due to high capital requirements. The *Staff Report* had come to a similar conclusion. The Federal Trade Commission, on appeal, ignored this testimony and supporting economic data, and reversed the Examiner's decision. The Commission based its decision upon a fear of possible foreclosure to potential entrants. The federal courts of appeal affirmed the Commission's decisions.

STRUCTURE CRITERIA:

In examining mergers and their effect on competition from a structural perspective, lawyers and economists look at the number of firms in a relevant market, the size of the firms, the nature of the product and obstacles to entry.

In the economist prepared *Staff Report,* emphasis is placed on regional and metropolitan markets in evaluating the degree of concentration (percentage of market controlled by a few firms) in the cement industry. The *Report* states that each metropolitan market has *unique* demand and supply characteristics based on distribution costs, competing suppliers and local trends in construction activity. In both the *U.S. Steel* and *Mississippi* cases, the appellate courts concluded that geographic markets should be defined as the area to which the purchaser can practically turn for supplies. The two firms argued that their markets were *unique* due to the nature of their locations and the actual competition involved. Mississippi particularly noted the access to a waterway at St. Louis and Memphis available to competing firms in arguing for a regional market. In both cases, however, the appellate court accepted the full Commission's view that concentration ratios were to be based on narrow metropolitan areas despite the defendant's arguments and the hearing examiner's findings that the New York (U.S. Steel), St. Louis and Memphis markets (Mississippi) had special characteristics which provided for a broader market.

In these cases, the examiners, in their initial decisions, concluded that the acquisitions would not significantly increase concentration even in the narrow metropolitan markets. Findings were based on statistical evidence as to market shares and concentration ratios. In *U.S. Steel,* the Examiner found that the UAC Division of U.S. Steel (cement producer) accounted for 11.4 percent of cement shipped into New York market in the year 1964 (the acquisition of Certified Industries taking place in 1963). The acquired company, Certified, accounted for nine percent of the cement consumed by ready mix companies in the New York market in that year. The examiner noted that the U.S. Steel figures contrast sharply with Colonial Co., Inc.'s sales (its closest competitor) which accounted for thirty-one percent of cement shipments. Both the Commission and the federal court of appeals rejected the findings of the Examiner and cited previous cases where mergers resulted in acquired companies obtaining in excess of a thirty percent share of the market and an increase of thirty-three percent in concentration. The Court of Appeals stated that it only had to find a *probability* of lessening competition under Section 7 of the Clayton Act. The empirical data provided by economists on behalf of both the FTC staff and the two companies as to shares of the market and concentration ratios was ignored while relying on precedent and a strict interpretation of statutory language.

PERFORMANCE CRITERIA:

The test of effective or workable competition is the market place result. Economists advocate that such factors as the level of prices, profit rates, increased efficiency and innovation should be considered by the courts in evaluating mergers. Economists argue that firms can engage in predatory conduct or bring about increased concentration in acquiring another firm, yet the net result may be lower prices, more efficient production, innovation and a healthier industry. Thus, they conclude that the use of conduct and structure criteria alone may bring about an imperfect result because all variables have not been considered.

The *Staff Report* prepared by the Economic Research Bureau of the Commission found that cement prices had declined slightly in 1960 and 1967, although price changes had not moved uniformly in all areas. It found that in the Northeast prices had declined in the 1960's as much as twenty-five percent as a result of such techniques as prompt payment and "phantom delivery point" discounts. At the same time the *Report* found that profit levels since 1958 had been declining, noting that because of the relatively high level of fixed costs associated with cement production, there is a close correlation between the industry rate of capacity utilization and profitability.

In both the *U.S. Steel* and the *Mississippi* cases, the hearing examiners took note of a decrease in prices in the relevant geographic markets being litigated. In the *U.S. Steel* case, the examiner found that the largest reduction in prices in the New York market had taken place since 1960 and pointed to the testimony of expert witnesses that such a trend would continue with a stronger vertically integrated competitor. In ruling in favor of the U.S. Steel acquisition, the examiner cited the *Staff Report* analysis that cement companies having their own outlets have a better opportunity to increase plant utilization and reduction in per unit product cost. Then, in both cases, the Commission overruled the examiner's showing of improved performance arguing that the foreclosure of possible entrants from these markets was of more importance to the public interest.

In the *U.S. Steel* case, despite affirming the commission's decision, the Court of Appeals agreed that vertical integration created better levels of plant utilization and resulted in elimination of significant sales and marketing expenses. It also noted that cost savings resulted from the ability to integrate storage and distribution facilities of cement and ready mix operations into a single urban terminal. Then ignoring both the examiners and its own findings of better overall performance as a result of the merger of a cement manufacturer and mix-concrete producer, the court fell back on history and precedent, citing cases in unrelated industries.

In both cases examined in this chapter, the courts concluded, that in industries tending toward oligopoly, price cuts are often used by leading firms to punish an aggressive marketeer and to "woo away" crucial accounts of non-integrated firms. Witnesses from independent cement firms testified to the contrary, in regard to the cement industry. The courts of appeal ignored the findings of the examiners that no such leverage had ever been applied, and found that the capacity to lessen competition was the important concern under Section 7 of the Clayton Act. Of particular interest in both cases was the ability of competing independent ready-mix concrete companies to meet a possible reduction in price granted by the two companies to its acquired subsidiaries. Dr. Martin Seiden, an economist, testified that competing independent ready-mix concrete companies would turn to their cement suppliers to meet the challenge, noting that in several markets cement suppliers had already done so. Counsel for Mississippi, citing the *Staff Report* finding that information as to any reduction in prices is immediately known by competitors, argued that competition and overall performance would be enhanced if reductions such as these did take place. Both the Commission and the Courts of Appeal ignored the firms' arguments and expert testimony.

SUMMARY OF ANTITRUST REGULATION IN THE CEMENT INDUSTRY

The Commission and the courts of appeal used conduct and structure criteria to the exclusion of performance criterion. Economic inputs into decision-making at the Commission and courts of appeal level were ignored in favor of a strict interpretation of Section 7 of the Clayton Act based on previous cases in unrelated industries. Findings of the examiners as to conduct, structure and performance were either ignored or given little weight. A regulatory policy which applied the Clayton Act to the cement industry without consideration of performance criterion has led today to increased concentration and decreasing profit rates in the industry.[5] Legal analysis operating without consideration of the economic variables has brought decreased competition to the cement industry which is contrary to the professed goals of antitrust regulation.[6]

EVALUATION OF LAW AND ECONOMICS CONTRIBUTIONS TO REGULATORY POLICY

The law of trade regulation (inclusive of antitrust) is an interdisciplinary field dominated by lawyers and economists. Both disciplines contribute models and techniques for solutions of problems like the merger question illustrated in this chapter. What has been found is that neither law or economics operating independently contributes to an antitrust policy which brings about positive results for the companies and industries that are the object of its workings, or the public which is supposed to benefit from greater competition and decreased prices.

The case-by-case approach favored by lawyers using conduct-structural criteria for evaluating mergers tends to ignore the results following the decision, and limits analysis to the companies involved in the litigation. The agency or court fails to look at total industry performance and the effect (particularly economic) its decision may have on all in that industry. Because the legal process involves two or more adversaries, by its nature it tends to bring a micro perspective to problems that may need macro analysis. For this reason, it is believed by many lawyers as well as economists that the adversary legal model is not the correct structure for analyzing and providing solutions to antitrust problems.

The workable competition concept is favored by industrial organization economists, and has gained some credibility with the legal community. But agencies and courts still find it more comfortable and less uncertain to fall back on previous cases for support of their decisions rather than to rely on economic forecasting and econometric models. If performance criteria as outlined in this chapter are to be decisive considerations in decision-making, economic forecasting must be more exact and economic variables will have to be better controlled in an econometric model. Also, there will have to be more agreement among economists in predicting how a firm will perform and what effect an approved merger will have on the market and industry. Lawyers often accuse economists of being "hired guns" who will provide data and analysis for either side in return for their expert witness fees.

This dichotomy of models and goals for regulation between law and economics continues with law trained decision-makers using economic data which supports pre-ordained decisions. This allows for little analysis of long term economic results on an industry-wide basis, and often leads to increased concentration rather than more competition.

Mr. Justice Holmes was prophetic for antitrust regulation when he expressed his concern over the divorce between the disciplines of law and economics some eighty-two years ago. He may well have been correct when he stated: "For the rational study of the law, the blackletter man may be the man of the present; but the man of the future is the man of statistics and the master of economics."[7]

ENDNOTES

1. Mason, *Monopoly In Law and Economics,* 47 YALE L.J. 34 (1937). See also Mason, *The Current Status of the Monopoly Problem in the United States,* 62 **Har.L.Rev.** 1265 (1949). These writings represent the earliest attempts in this country to analyze the dichotomy of legal and economic thought.
2. **FTC, Economic Report on Mergers and Vertical Integration in the Cement Industry** 103 (1966).
3. Mississippi River Corporation v. FTC, 454 F.2d 1083 (8th Cir. 1972).
4. U.S. Steel Corporation v. FTC, 426 F.2d 592 (6th Cir. 1970).
5. See Allen, *Vertical Integration and Market Foreclosure: The Case of Cement and Concrete,* (1972), 14(1) **The Journal of Law and Economics** 251, 260 Table 2. An updating of Allen's computation based on United States Bureau of Mines Mineral Yearbook shows a general decline in profit rates. It should be noted that declines are traced from 1967 onward but shifts in the economy relating to housing have to be considered as well as the tough antitrust regulation the industry was subjected to.
6. See **J. Blair, Economic Concentration: Structure, Behavior and Public Policy,** 563 (1972) for other examples of the perverse effects of conduct-structure oriented commission and court decisions requiring dissolution or divestiture.
7. Holmes, *The Path of the Law, 10* **Har.L.Rev.,** 451, 469.

10

Forty-Five Years of Corporate Disclosure Regulation in Perspective

Jeremy Wiesen*

Many businesspersons have become more vocal about their distaste for the "paperwork" required by the U.S. government. A major example of paperwork is the information about companies which must be made available to shareholders and potential investors.

Corporate disclosure regulations affect only public companies—basically, corporations whose shares are publicly traded. Corporate disclosure is mainly required (1) when securities are issued for the first time, and (2) on an annual, quarterly and current basis to keep investors informed.

Each year hundreds of millions of dollars of the U.S. Gross National Product goes to accountants, lawyers, corporate executives and employees, members of the financial community, printers and government regulators in order to: (1) prepare reports required by the Securities and Exchange Commission (SEC), (2) defend lawsuits when a violation of corporate disclosure regulation is alleged, and (3) structure management of the corporation in a way that will increase the likelihood that accurate reports will be issued.

There has been some progress in reducing the paperwork imposed by the federal bureaucracy on business. Almost independent of this effort, several groups have been making fundamental evaluations of the efficacy of corporate disclosure regulation. Therefore, this is an appropriate time to take a perspective on the forty-five years of corporate disclosure regulation, and to attempt to predict its future direction. Most businesspersons in the U.S., and many abroad, will be affected by these developments.

The Securities Act of 1933 ("the Securities Act," "the 1933 Act") was passed by Congress in response to highly publicized securities fraud scandals. The Act requires a company to file a "registration statement" with the SEC when it offers to sell its securities (defined broadly, to include stocks, bonds, etc.) to the public. The SEC does not pass judgment as to whether the securities are a sound investment; rather, the SEC only makes an attempt to assure that there

---

*New York University

is full and fair disclosure in the registration statement, and in a prospectus (basically the registration statement, without the appendices) distributed to purchasers of the securities. The 1933 Act makes the issuing company, its directors and officers (who signed the registration statement), underwriters (who helped sell the offering to the public), and the accountants (who audited the financial statements) liable to investors for losses if the registration statement or prospectus contains materially misleading statements.

One year after passage of the Securities Act, Congress enacted the Securities Exchange Act of 1934 ("the Exchange Act," "the 1934 Act"). With the 1933 Act, the two statutes are known as the Securities Acts. Congress has since passed four more securities-related statutes, but they are more specialized, regulating business enterprises such as mutual funds and utility holding companies.

The 1934 Act created the SEC (for one year the 1933 Act had been administered by the Federal Trade Commission). The Exchange Act, as its name indicates, also contains provisions for regulating the securities exchanges, such as the New York Stock Exchange. More relevant to corporate disclosure regulation are the following provisions of the 1934 Act:

- Publicly traded companies must file annual, and other periodic reports. The annual report must contain audited financial statements.
- Publicly traded companies above a certain size must issue proxy statements to shareholders to permit them to vote at shareholder meetings without being there. The proxies must contain full and fair disclosure, and must include certain proposals submitted by shareholders for vote at the meeting.
- Purchases and sales of securities must not involve materially misleading information, or any other kind of fraud or deceit.

This background makes it possible to analyze, in a broad way, the past, present and future of U.S. corporate disclosure regulation.

THE PAST

REGISTRATION OF PRIMARY SECURITIES OFFERINGS

For the first 30 years of existence, corporate disclosure regulation mainly focused on the content of 1933 Act registration statements and the scope of the few exemptions from registration. The SEC typically brought "stop-order" proceedings to halt the "effectiveness" of registration statements on the grounds that full and fair disclosure had not been made. Today stop-order proceedings are not common.

In the early 1960s the SEC's focus on new offerings of securities began to shift. Professors of law and finance began to contend that the disclosure emphasis for companies already public should be on their annual reports, interim reports, and news releases rather than on the registration of offerings of new securities. By the early 1970s, the SEC began to increase the required content of the periodic reports, particularly the annual report filed with the SEC (Form 10-K) and the annual report to shareholders, while allowing registration statements for offerings of securities of companies already public to be more abbreviated through incorporation by reference of information in 1934 Act reports.

In 1974 the SEC ended its long-held objection to the inclusion of projections (forecasts) of earnings in SEC-filed statements. The SEC had been concerned that companies, especially when offering securities to the public, would issue overly-optimistic forecasts. The SEC is now considering ways to encourage projections by absolving a company from liability if its forecast is competently prepared but is later shown to have been inaccurate. The SEC is also considering the suitability of other types of "soft," future-oriented information which may be of utility to investors.

In changing its focus of attention, the SEC is responding to some of the recommendations of the Advisory Committee on Corporate Disclosure (the Sommer Committee). For example, the committee's report, issued in 1977, recommends that the SEC create one Continuous Disclosure (CD) report which could be used for all 1933 and 1934 Act filings (although not all items in the report would be required for each filing). Furthermore, the SEC may be anticipating recommendations of the American Law Institute which will soon propose a bill to Congress that combines the 1933 and 1934 Acts. The new act de-emphasizes a public company's offering of securities and thus further demotes the once leading aspect of corporate disclosure regulation—the registration of offerings of new securities.

INSIDER TRADING AND TIPPING

In 1961 the SEC began an attempt to control insider trading and tipping (improperly revealing inside information) through an administrative opinion against a brokerage house. Its drive was significantly bolstered in 1968 by the famous Court of Appeals decision in *SEC v. Texas Gulf Sulphur Co.*

Wall Street and corporations were alarmed. The SEC was moving abruptly to regulate a new area not specifically addressed in the Securities Acts, using the argument that business was acting unethically. Furthermore, the SEC, or at least its staff, did not seem very concerned that the livelihood of an entire profession (security analysts) was threatened. Businesspersons saw an omen in the fact that the SEC's Division of Enforcement was in charge of this matter rather than the Division of Corporation Finance which had been the kingpin when the SEC's primary concern was registration statements.

At the height of interest in insider trading and tipping at least one hundred law review articles discussed the complex legal nuances burdening securities lawyers, corporate managers and judges. Such issues included the meaning of "materiality," "insider," "inside information," and the proper duties of security analysts.

These issues have still not been resolved, but hardly anyone is complaining because SEC and shareholder suits involving the misuse of inside information are no longer a significant threat to business. The SEC and New York Stock Exchange suits against Raymond Dirks, the security analyst who tipped information about the Equity Funding fraud, have been lingering for several years. Wall Street firms are no longer very concerned about the conflicting legal obligations to construct "Chinese Walls" around underwriting departments so that inside information does not leak out, while at the same time permitting securities salesmen to have access to some of the information. The SEC has not issued guidelines on the "digestion period" for corporate news before insiders may tip or trade, even though the court in the 1968 *Texas Gulf Sulphur* case suggested it do so; nor has the SEC issued the comprehensive guidelines on inside information problems for which it solicited comments from the public in 1973.

The lack of concern with legal issues does not mean that businesspersons are misusing inside information with impunity. The SEC has been able to impose a degree of self-regulation on business by "encouraging" corporations and Wall Street firms to adopt internal guidelines for the proper handling of inside information. The guidelines were set forth in the provisions of SEC settled lawsuits (consent decrees), and SEC commissioner and staff speeches advocated that others adopt similar internal policies. As a warning that government suits based on insider trading and tipping were still possible, in early 1978 the SEC cooperated with the Justice Department in bringing the first criminal case based on the misuse of inside information.

However, today the SEC's enforcement staff has clearly shifted its interest to other issues (described below) and the head of that division recently admitted that it was very difficult for the SEC to investigate all instances of alleged misuse of inside information brought to its attention. Reluctantly, he provided statistics to support his point. This was a complete turn from the SEC staff's attitude in the late 1960s and early 1970s—that insider trading and tipping must, and will, be stopped. Also a vigorous pursuit of insider cases has been stymied by recent court decisions that have made it more difficult for the SEC and private parties to win suits based on the general antifraud provisions of the 1934 Act, particularly suits which seek an injunction against insider trading and tipping.

THE PRESENT

The present state of corporate disclosure regulation does not make a complete break from past issues, nor does it exclude elements of future regulation, which are discussed in the next section.

At present Congress and the SEC are concerned with the extent to which the accounting profession should be more closely regulated by the SEC, or regulated by a new administrative agency. Also commanding the SEC's attention are six Supreme Court cases between 1974-1977 which were adverse to SEC positions. These decisions narrowed the definition of a security, limited standing to sue under the Securities Acts, and removed the possibility of using the main antifraud provision in the 1934 Act when only mere negligence can be proven. However, the present is still dominated by the effects of one issue: the *Corporate Payments Scandal* (hereinafter "the CPS").

CORPORATE PAYMENTS SCANDAL

The CPS has had world-wide consequences—for example politicians and royalty in several countries have had to vacate their positions. The uncovering of the scandal can be attributed chiefly to the SEC and its regulation of corporate disclosure. The SEC's enforcement staff, like millions of Americans, listened in 1974 to the Senate Watergate hearings, which concerned the break-in at the Democratic party's Watergate offices. The SEC staff heard testimony that the Republican party regularly received secret donations from corporations in order to avoid the limitations on the maximum amount that corporations could contribute to political parties. The donated money had been "laundered" by the corporations, i.e., it lost its identity by being deposited in secret bank accounts in Switzerland, the Bahamas and elsewhere. On the premise that Congress must have "intended" the Securities Acts would prohibit such conduct, the SEC brought suit against a few corporations, alleging secret political payments. Soon thereafter, the front pages of newspapers carried the story of Eli Black, president of United Brands jumping to his death from his office window. The SEC began a routine informal investigation and found that a reason for the suicide was the possible disclosure of United Brands' secret bribes to Central American political officials in order to expedite the importation of fruit and to reduce the taxes paid by United Brands in those countries. The corporate payments scandal soon came to occupy substantial SEC time.

The impact of the CPS on corporate disclosure regulation can be summarized in the following four categories:

MATERIALITY

Not all information about a company needs to be reported to shareholders and potential investors. For example, a shareholder cannot validly complain that he was not informed that the main plant of the company was painted. Corporate disclosure regulation pursuant to the Securities Act is limited to *material* information. Corporate officials assert that the SEC cannot require the disclosure of most secret corporate payments for political or foreign bribes, because the amounts are usually small compared to the sales or earnings of the company.

The SEC's chief argument, which is now an established concept in corporate disclosure regulation, is that information which affects the integrity of management, or the integrity of the company's books and records, is material even if the dollar amount is very small. Secret corporate payments have, at the least, usually involved some mislabeling of accounts in the books and records and, therefore, the SEC contends that the transactions are generally material.

SELF-INVESTIGATIONS AND CODES OF CONDUCT

Before the CPS, in a few egregious cases, the SEC had settled suits by requiring the defendant companies to appoint "independent" persons to investigate the full extent of wrongdoing. These in-house investigators were either outside directors of the company or specially-hired lawyers and accountants.

A committee of the board of directors, such as an audit committee, was often assigned the responsibility of overseeing the investigation.

The development of this tool as an adjunct to the SEC's own enforcement work became the crux of the SEC's handling of the CPS. The SEC could never have managed to send its investigators out to the hundreds of companies it suspected of having made illegal domestic or foreign payments. Instead, the SEC established a formal "voluntary disclosure program" in which almost 400 companies participated. They conducted independent internal investigations, made the information available to the SEC, and at the same time, disclosed a summary of the information to investors.

The SEC's program also required the development of corporate codes of conduct which prohibit illegal payments, require proper record keeping, and prohibit the use of inside information and other types of unethical conduct. The codes also provide for compliance and monitoring the procedures. Some persons view the codes as corporate bibles and as in-house extensions of the Securities Acts.

INDEPENDENT DIRECTORS AND AUDIT COMMITTEES

Most of the internal investigations were supervised by independent directors and audit committees. Until the CPS there were only two kinds of directors of U.S. corporations: inside and outside directors. Inside directors are officers—full-time employees of the corporation. Outside directors are all other directors. In the CPS, the SEC developed the concept of *independent* outside directors—directors who had absolutely no contact with the company other than being on the board. Under this definition lawyers, consultants and bankers for the company are outside directors, but they are not independent directors, and so the company cannot rely on them to fulfill such needs as internal investigations. The term independent may require that friends of management be excluded from that category of directors.

The SEC suggests that boards of directors establish audit committees comprised solely of independent directors, and most large companies have done so. These committees meet with the company's independent (outside) auditors, and with the company's internal auditors, to discuss the annual audit of the company. This procedure aids independent directors in checking the financial information being disseminated by the company by enabling them to study the process which generated it.

The New York Stock Exchange now requires all of its listed companies to have audit committees. Congress and the SEC are considering requiring all publicly traded companies to have them. The American Institute of Certified Public Accountants is considering the prohibition of audits of companies which do not have audit committees.

RECORD-KEEPING AND INDEPENDENT AUDITORS

The main lesson the SEC wants businesspersons to learn from the CPS is that books and records must be accurately maintained in order for a company's financial statements to be relied upon by stockholders and investors. In response to the CPS, Congress passed the Foreign Corrupt Practices Act of

1977, which prohibits making false entries in the books and records of publicly traded companies.

Congress, the SEC and others have asked why independent auditors failed to uncover or disclose the false entries which concealed secret foreign and domestic payments. There is no definitive answer at this time; but, simply posing the question has moved auditors to assume greater responsibilities. The auditing profession has adopted new standards which require an awareness of the possibility of illegal management conduct, which require a further investigation if such conduct is uncovered, and, which give greater significance to the auditor's evaluation of the company's internal control procedures. Auditors are presently considering whether to insist that boards of directors adopt an adequate code of conduct.

CORPORATE "PERKS"

In 1977, the SEC issued a release which stated that officers and directors should not fail to include the value of corporate perquisite—such as company-paid vacations and company cars for personal use—in required disclosures of officer and director remuneration. Few, if any, corporate managers had been valuing and including such "perks." As a check on your understanding of the effects of the CPS, can you describe the effects that a "perks scandal" can have on corporate disclosure regulation?

The effects are the following:
1. Companies will have to accept the SEC's regulation of perks.
2. Perks information will have to be considered material even if it concerns relatively small dollar amounts.
3. Audit committees should investigate management representations of perks for the current year.
4. Directors should consider investigating the extent to which perks were not disclosed in past years.
5. Corporate codes of conduct should include a provision which bars the receipt of unauthorized perks, and which requires the disclosure of all perks, authorized and unauthorized.
6. Independent auditors must consider their role regarding perks disclosures.

THE FUTURE

THE NON-INVESTOR MOVEMENT

Corporate disclosure regulation appears to be moving away from merely providing information to investors, and instead, toward becoming an instrument for social regulation. This trend has five aspects:
1. *Corporate Governance.* Ralph Nader and others have asserted that companies are "undemocratic" because management directors are able to nominate themselves or their friends to the board of directors. The only way a shareholder can effectively nominate another person for a directorship is by waging an expensive proxy fight.

Congress and the SEC responded to these and other assertions by holding public hearings on corporate governance in 1977. It is not clear what solutions will emerge, but most reform proposals involve the corporate disclosure machinery as a means for allowing shareholders to have a greater control over boards of directors. The aim here is not to improve corporate earnings or to increase corporate dividends, but rather to make U.S. companies more responsible, more accountable and more democratic. Thus, this is part of a *non-investor movement*.

2. Social activists are satisfied that the SEC requires many shareholders' social accountability proposals to be included in management's proxy material. Also significant, a federal court has persisted in forcing the SEC to consider requiring companies to include information on social accountability in statements filed with the SEC.

3. The SEC and Congress are concerned with the number of "takeovers" of large companies (by other large companies), especially takeovers by foreign companies. Similarly, the SEC and the Delaware state courts are moving to close off the possibility of "unfair squeeze-outs'" of minority shareholders when a company "goes private."

4. The SEC and state courts have shown indications of requiring officers and directors to manage companies with greater financial and managerial sophistication. The ultimate aim may be to improve the allocation of capital in the U.S., with the vehicle being corporate disclosure regulation.

5. There are signs that corporate disclosure regulation will be used by workers to attempt to achieve co-determination in the running of U.S. corporations. Employee groups have begun to present to shareholders their aspirations for higher wages and for representation on corporate boards by having such matters included in management proxies. Employees own many shares of U.S. companies through pension funds, and it seems likely that corporate disclosure regulation will be further used by workers to promote their objectives.

11

Advertising and the Federal Trade Commission

O. Lee Reed, Jr.*

In a series of dramatic decisions in the mid-1970's, the United States Supreme Court declared that advertising was "protected speech" under the First Amendment. Thus ended a nearly forty-year period in American history during which the judiciary largely excluded commercial expression from the freedom of expression guarantees of the Constitution. The $30-billion-a-year advertising industry hailed the Court's decisions as potent ammunition for the industry's continuing battles with its chief regulatory adversary — the Federal Trade Commission. To what extent this view is justified is one of the topics covered in this chapter on the regulation of advertising by the FTC. Also discussed are the Commission's early history, some examples of deception, a procedural case study, and several important trends in advertising regulation.

Throughout our nation's history, advertising has played an important role in the communication between sellers and buyers. Founding fathers George Washington and Benjamin Franklin both used advertising to promote their business activities. In spite of the importance of advertising to the private enterprise system, however, the public has not always appreciated the role of advertising in our economic process. Because of the *caveat emptor* (let the buyer beware) views which prevailed in the courts prior to this century, the common law remedies which buyers could apply against false and misleading advertising were woefully inadequate, and during the 1800's commercial falsehoods became a staple of advertising practice. As the public increasingly lost confidence in the truthfulness of advertising, reputable advertisers in the early 1900's began to press for legislation to limit advertising's excesses in hope of restoring public trust.

One of the first such pieces of legislation was the famous *Printer's Ink* statute of 1912, which was named for the trade journal that sponsored it. Widely adopted by the states, the statute made false and misleading advertising a criminal misdemeanor. While of interest to historians, the statute had

*University of Georgia

little impact on advertising practices since it was seldom applied. Of greater import for the regulation of advertising was the passage in 1914 of national legislation establishing the Federal Trade Commission.

HISTORY OF THE FTC

EARLY HISTORY

Perhaps the most important development in the FTC's early regulation of advertising was that the Commission concerned itself with advertising in the first place. The legislative history of the Federal Trade Commission Act of 1914 reveals that Congress in passing the Act was not interested in the regulation of advertising. Instead, the FTC Act was the response of Congress to the hostility of the courts, especially the Supreme Court, toward enforcement of the Sherman Antitrust Act. Congress envisioned its newly created agency, which was endowed with powers not only from the FTC Act but from the simultaneously enacted Clayton Antitrust Act, as primarily a tool for addressing anticompetitive restraints on trade.

From the very beginning, however, the FTC initiated actions against false advertising, which has remained a favorite target of the Commission in the intervening decades. In the first year of its existence, the FTC issued only five complaints, of which three involved false advertising—the labeling of cotton as silk. As odd as the Commission's early emphasis on false advertising may appear in light of the congressional purpose for the FTC, there was actually a rational basis for such an emphasis: The Commission viewed false advertisements as being "unfair methods of competition" against one's competitiors and considered that such advertisements contributed to the formation of monopoly. A secondary and somewhat more cynical reason for the Commission's concern with false advertising must have been that it was much easier, then as now, to prosecute false advertising cases instead of grappling with complex monopoly or restraint of trade issues.

In early decisions the courts almost invariably upheld the FTC's interpretation of "unfair competition" as including false and misleading advertising. In fact while the courts upheld on appeal only forty-three of eighty-two Commission orders from 1914 to 1931, they affirmed twenty-two of the twenty-nine orders prohibiting false advertisements. In 1931, however, the unanimous Supreme Court held in *FTC* v. *Raladam* that the FTC could not ban false advertisements which affected only consumers and did not hurt the advertiser's competitors. The Court's ruling set the stage for an amendment to the FTC Act which greatly increased the Commission's power to regulate advertising.

WHEELER-LEA AMENDMENT

Following the 1931 *Raladam* decision, the FTC's regulation of commercial expression was limited to those false and misleading advertisements which adversely affected "competition." Consumers were protected only incidentally as a by-product of the Commission's efforts to prevent the false advertiser from injuring its competitors. In 1938, however, Congress through the Wheeler-Lea Amendment expanded the Commission's statutory authority to protect consumers as well as competitors from advertising abuses. Interestingly, one reason the FTC received this expanded power was because advertisers, who saw they could not stop such consumer-oriented legislation, successfully lobbied Congress to grant the power to the Federal Trade Commission instead of to the Food and Drug Administration which was viewed by the advertisers as being the more effective of the two agencies.

The Wheeler-Lea Amendment added the phrase "unfair or deceptive acts or practices" to the FTC Act's original prohibition in Sec. 5 against "unfair methods of competition." Making it clear that the amendment's purpose was to protect consumers, one Congressional report on the amendment stated: "This amendment makes the consumer, who may be injured by unfair trade practices, of equal concern before the law, with the merchant or manufacturer injured by the unfair methods of a dishonest competitor." The report also specified that one of the practices against which the FTC was to protect consumers was false and misleading advertising: "We cannot ignore the evils and abuses of advertising; the imposition upon the unsuspecting; and the downright criminality of preying upon the sick as well as the consuming public through fradulent, false, or subtle misleading advertisements." Congress had come to share the Commission's concern over advertising practices in the years between 1914 and 1938.

In passing the amendment Congress realized that attempting to enumerate and define the types of advertising practices to be forbidden would be futile. Instead, Congress intended the FTC to possess authority

> broad enough to cover every form of advertisement deception over which it would be humanly practicable to exercise governmental control. It covers every case of imposition on a purchaser for which there could be a practical remedy. It reaches every case from that of inadvertant or uninformed advertising to that of the most subtle as well as most vicious types of advertisement.

Thus, the FTC was granted the broadest possible powers to regulate the practices of advertisers.

While the Wheeler-Lea Amendment authorized the Commission to regulate unfair *or* deceptive advertisements until recently the Commission has focused almost exclusively upon advertisements it determines to be "deceptive" to consumers. This emphasis on developing the doctrine of deception as contained in Sec. 5, instead of on developing a doctrine of unfairness, becomes understandable in light of the legal history of the word *deception*. We must also take into consideration that the FTC regulators have nearly all been lawyers.

In the common law, which was developed by judges over several centuries, "deception" has the same meaning as "fraud". To commit an act of legal deception at common law requires (1) the making of an intentional misrepresentation of material fact (or failure to disclose material fact in certain instances) (2) which is justifiably believed and acted upon by someone (3) to his or her injury. At common law, legal deception is both an actionable tort and ground for rescission of a contract based on the misrepresentation.

Congress charged the Commission with interpreting the broad language of Sec. 5. The Commission looked to the common law meaning of deception in applying Sec. 5 of the FTC Act. As the early commissioners were almost all lawyers they naturally examined the legal history of the words which granted their powers. Since there was a legal history of what is "deceptive" to consumers while there was not a corresponding legal history of what might be considered "unfair" to consumers, the lawyers on the commission emphasized regulation of deceptive advertising practices and devoted little attention to advertisements which might be characterized as unfair. Although the distinction between the words *unfair* and *deceptive* may seem nit-picking to the average layperson, this distinction becomes important later in the chapter when we consider the regulation of advertising through the electronic media.

Although the FTC's regulation of advertising has been significantly colored by the common law meaning of deception, the Commission's view of what constitutes statutory deception in advertising has evolved away from the strict common law model of deception. The FTC's regulatory actions in the "public interest" have demanded a different application of the deception doctrine than that known at common law between private individuals. For example, in the FTC's regulation of advertising which misleads and misrepresents, there is no legal requirement, as there is at common law, that the Commission establish that the advertiser *intended* to misrepresent the product or service. A simple showing of misrepresentation is sufficient. Likewise, the Commission need not demonstrate that specific consumers have actually believed and acted upon the misrepresentation to their injury. All the Commission need conclude is that a challenged advertisement has the "tendency" or the "capacity" to deceive consumers by inducing them to rely on the misrepresentation.

EXAMPLES OF TRADITIONAL DECEPTION

As mentioned previously, it is not possible to enumerate and define every type of advertisement which the FTC may choose to call deceptive. Even so, by looking at the kinds of practices the Commission traditionally has condemned as deceptive, we are able to identify several occasionally overlapping categories into which deceptive advertisements may be placed. It is important, however, to emphasize that these categories are fixed for convenience's sake, and they should not be taken to limit the Commission's power to define deception.

PRODUCT NAMES AND DESIGNATIONS

Advertisers who are alert to consumer preferences will sometimes designate their products deceptively in order to take advantage of these preferences. There are a number of cases in which the FTC has acted to prevent misleading and deceptive product designations.

Thus, in one action the FTC forbade an advertiser to advertise or identify its product as a "hard rubber" comb when in fact the comb was made of a synthetic compound which included rubber. The Commission acted to preserve the meaningfulness of consumer preference for "hard rubber" and, not incidentally, to protect other advertisers who were selling hard rubber combs. Similarly, the Commission has held it deceptive for a seller to fail to designate his product as "re-refined oil" when selling motor oil which had been refined, used, then re-refined for sale again. The FTC found deception in this case in spite of the fact that re-refined oil is indistinguishable from oil which has been refined only once. The Commission deemed that it ruled properly because of customer bias, however irrational, against re-refined oil.

Other product designation cases have concerned the deceptiveness of advertising "French" perfume which was not made in France, "California white pine" which was actually yellow pine, and a "Hong Kong" rug which carried a tag correctly indicating it was made in Italy. In each of these cases, the Commission ruled that deception existed.

DESCRIPTION OF PRODUCT QUALITIES AND QUANTITIES

Although there exist an infinity of deceptive ways to describe a product, several more common ones can be pinpointed. Claims of deceptive uniqueness have often been attacked by the FTC. Thus, sellers have been forced in specific cases to give up such product descriptions as "best," "pre-eminent," "finest in America," and "purest," even though casual observation reveals that these and other product descriptions still abound.

Deceptive descriptions of product function comprise another common category of advertisement traditionally regulated by the FTC. In one of the best known such cases, the Commission restrained an advertiser from describing its product by name as a "Rejuvenescence Cream." The Commission concluded that rejuvenescence was medically impossible.

The Commission also has found deceptive overemphasis of insignificant facts about a product. Thus, one advertiser was forced to change the name of its product, Butt-R-Milk Soap, when it was discovered to contain only a trace of buttermilk. The Commission required another advertiser to cease describing a liquid roofing product as *asbestos* because it contained too little asbestos to retard materially the chance of fire.

If an advertiser describes a product ambiguously so that the description has two meanings, one truthful and one misleading, the advertisement containing the description is deceptive. For example, in certain medical claims cases the words "remedy for," "overcomes," "eliminates," "clears away," and "puts an end to," were held to suggest that advertised products would cure some particular condition. Since the products merely gave relief, not cure, the usage of these words was deceptive, according to the Commission.

Deception in product quantity description has been the object of a special statute broadening and defining FTC powers. Under the Fair Packaging and Labeling Act of 1966, Congress authorized the FTC to regulate the use of quantity descriptions such as *huge, large, giant,* etc., and to set standardization of product container sizes when proliferation of sizes renders consumer selection difficult.

PRICE INFORMATION

In recognition of P.T. Barnum's cynical observation that "a sucker is born every minute," the Federal Trade Commission has attacked advertisements which mislead prospective buyers into believing that they are getting something for nothing when such is not the case. The Commission has ruled it deceptive to advertise products as "on sale" at lower than the "regular price" unless the advertiser has usually sold the product at that price. Likewise, the Commisson has enjoined advertisements which offer items for sale at "two-for-the-price-of-one," when there has been no customary selling price for a single item. "Buy-one-get-one-free" advertisements raise similar problems when the selling price of the purchased product is raised from the usual price.

SALES PROMOTIONS

The FTC has interdicted as deceptive various kinds of sales promotions or schemes. One of the most familiar deceptive sales promotions is illegal baiting. "Baiting" consumers into a retail store by advertising the availability of an item which is unavailable for sale injures not only consumers but also the advertiser's honest competitors and is decidedly deceptive. Similarly, the Commission prohibits the practice of "baiting-and-switching," i.e. of luring customers into the seller's place of business by advertising that goods or services are for sale when the seller does not intend to sell them but rather to switch the customers to other, generally higher priced, goods or services.

Another illegal promotional scheme is the disguise of a sale in a form likely to entice consumers: for example, the advertisement of seemingly unqualified gifts which actually require a purchase. Under certain circumstances the advertisement of an employment opportunity may also be illegal if it later turns out to be coupled with a sale (e.g., a sale of vending machines).

The use of mock-ups in advertisements presents special problems in promoting products. Many products do not film attractively, and the use of mock-ups may be legitimate. But the Commission has ruled mock-ups deceptive if their purpose is to present to the viewer objective proof of the claims made. In this vein the FTC has declared deceptive the use of plexiglass coated with sand in a "sandpaper-shaving" demonstration and also the filming of an automobile windshield to show clarity of glass when in fact the windshield had been removed from the automobile since glass does not film well. In recent years the FTC has filed fewer complaints involving deceptive mock-ups because their power to injure the consumers is unclear and because most advertisers currently identify mock-ups as such in sales promotions, thereby removing the possibility of deception.

TESTIMONIALS

The use of testimonial recommendations from athletic superstars and entertainment celebrities is extremely widespread in current advertising. Because potential purchasers rely on the opinions of well-known personalities with whom they identify, the FTC presently considers advertising deceptive when such individuals claim that they use and prefer advertised products when in actuality they do not. The Commission has issued guidelines to assist advertisers in avoiding deception in the use of testimonials.

A HYPOTHETICAL CASE STUDY

In one of his poems, Carl Sandberg asks the question: "Why does the hearse horse snicker hauling the lawyer away?" At least in part the answer lies in the fact that the legal process is bewildering, frustrating, and, finally, angering to the average layperson. This confusion and frustration is often especially intense to firms which must face the legal process as a defendant (called "respondent") in an action filed by a giant regulatory agency such as the FTC. To clarify the legal process involved in the FTC's regulation of advertising, we should examine the procedural course of a typical action brought against an advertiser. For this purpose a hypothetical case study involving the advertisements of a product named "Kisterine" has been constructed. Both the product and its advertiser are fictitious.

"Kisterine" is a mouth and throat wash manufactured by the Borg Manufacturing Co., a small, family-owned company which during the past three years has successfully penetrated the national market with television, radio, and print advertising for its mouthwash. Created by Borg's bright, young advertising manager, this advertising is directed at mothers with small children. It advises that in order to "protect" children from "sore throats during the upcoming cold season" mothers should have them use "Kisterine twice daily." These mothers are also told that "Kisterine kills *millions of germs* in the mouth." The advertising always concludes with the slogan "Mothers who care use Kisterine."

One day Borg unexpectedly receives notice that the "Kisterine" advertising campaign is under current investigation by the FTC since the advertisements allegedly "claim by implication and innuendo that Kisterine prevents and cures colds." Wondering why the FTC has come to investigate Borg's advertising, Borg's advertising manager immediately makes an appointment to see a lawyer who is a former Commission staff member now in private law practice.

The lawyer explains first that the FTC may begin investigation of an advertising practice following complaints by consumers, competitors of the advertiser, or governmental officials, and that the FTC also may undertake investigation on its own initiative as a result of an industry-wide study of advertising practices or on the recommendation of its media monitoring unit. Next he warns that the Commission possesses the legal power to compel Borg to furnish it with whatever information it deems necessary for its investigation. The lawyer further explains that the present investigation likely orginated within the FTC's Bureau of Consumer Protection, one of the Commission's three bureaus, and that if the Bureau concludes that the "Kisterine" campaign is illegally deceptive, it will use one of several procedures to bring the campaign to a halt: assurance of voluntary compliance, consent order, or adjudication by an administrative law judge leading to a cease-and-desist order.

The first of these procedures—assurance of voluntary compliance—may be used when the advertising practice has already ceased. After weighing whether or not the public interest will be adequately protected by voluntary cessation and considering "the nature and gravity of the alleged violation" and "the past record of good faith of the parties involved," the FTC may allow the advertiser to assure voluntarily that it will not continue the offending practice.

If the advertiser later breaks its promise of voluntary cessation, the FTC will resume its action against the advertiser, although no penalty arises from the broken promise.

Borg's advertising manager learns that if voluntary compliance is not permitted, the Commission staff will prepare a formal complaint against Borg. The staff will also inform the company that it intends to issue the complaint and that the advertiser has ten days to offer to accept a consent order, the second of the procedures mentioned above. Under the consent order, the advertiser does not admit that is is guilty of deception or unfairness, but it does formally and legally consent to stop the alleged illegality and to agree to whatever remedy the Commission imposes upon it. If the advertiser later breaks the consent order, it may be subject to judicial proceedings and a fine of up to $10,000 per day.

The lawyer further advises the manager that if a consent agreement is not reached or is considered to be against the public interest, the Commission staff will issue the complaint and prepare for a hearing on the complaint before an administrative law judge. (The administrative law judges are a branch of the judiciary within the FTC, and these judges hear exclusively cases brought by the FTC staff.) A hearing date will next be set, and upon that date the administrative law judge will render a decision on the complaint after hearing the evidence and witnesses presented by both parties. If the judge agrees with the Commission staff, who bear the burden of proving the violation, he (or she) will issue an order requiring the advertiser to "cease-and-desist" from the illegal practice and will impose whatever additional remedy is called for, such as a rebate to consumers or corrective advertising. As with the consent order, violation of a cease-and-desist order may bring a penalty of $10,000 per day.

Following the initial decision of the administrative law judge, either party (usually the one who loses) may appeal to the five commissioners who head the FTC. By majority vote the commissioners may affirm, modify, or reverse the judge's decision and order. This final decision by the commissioners does not become operative for sixty days to allow the respondent (advertiser) who loses to decide whether or not to appeal to the federal Court of Appeals.

At this point the lawyer is very careful to tell Borg's advertising manager that a successful appeal to the Court of Appeals is highly unlikely. The federal courts recognize that Congress mandated the Commission, not the courts, to decide what types of advertisements are unfair or deceptive. Bowing to the Commission's expertise and legislative grant of authority, the courts will overturn a Commission decision only if it is unsupported by "substantial evidence" (which is less than the "preponderance of the evidence" standard in civil cases) or if the Commission has exceeded its legislative authority or deprived the advertiser of its constitutional rights, e.g., freedom of speech or due process. The courts do not reweigh the evidence, hear new evidence, or substitute their view of the evidence for the Commission's. Practically, then, there is only a slender chance of obtaining a reversal of a Commission decision.

Lastly, Borg's advertising manager explores with the lawyer the possibility that the Commission will find deceptive the language of the "Kisterine" campaign. The manager argues that the real meaning of the advertising assertion that the product will "protect" children from "sore throats during the upcoming cold season" is not that it will prevent or cure colds, as the FTC alleges, but that it will relieve the pain of sore throats due to colds. Shaking his head, the lawyer explains that where the meaning of an advertisement is subject to two interpretations, one of which is deceptive, that the FTC will interpret the language against the advertiser and declare the entire advertisement deceptive.

When the manager points out that no consumer has ever complained to the company about the "Kisterine" advertising, the lawyer says that no such complaints are necessary. The Commission does not have to find that specific consumers have been deceived in order to prohibit the "Kisterine" commercials. The only requirement is for the Commission to find a "tendency or capacity" for deception to exist. Furthermore, the lawyer counsels, the "tendency or capacity" standard is not even applied to an "average" or "reasonable" person. It may also be applied to protect "the ignorant, the unthinking, and the credulous" as well as the "average" or "reasonable" person.

Upon leaving the lawyer's office, Borg's advertising manager has a much better understanding of the legal procedures followed by the FTC in challenging an advertising practice. When understood, the law is less fearsome and frustrating. Still, there are several additional factors which must be carefully weighed before the appropriate response to the Commission's challenge can be determined: the profit to Borg of continuing the "Kisterine" campaign while fighting and appealing any Commission ruling, the expense of the litigation, the possible loss of consumer goodwill arising out of a lengthy, highly-publicized battle with the Commission, the useful life-cycle of the product and the advertising campaign, and the difficulty of re-positioning "Kisterine" in the market should the present campaign be terminated. As of the time of this writing, the company has not yet reached a final decision on what its response should be.

RECENT TRENDS IN
FTC REGULATION OF ADVERTISING

In thinking about the FTC's regulatory activities, one should keep in mind that the Commission has a political nature as well as a legal one. The five commissioners who control the agency are appointed to staggered terms by the President. As might be expected, they tend to reflect the President's attitudes toward the regulation of advertising and other trade practices. In addition the FTC must look to Congress each year for its funding and is consequently responsive to the prevailing political moods of that body. Thus, new regulatory emphases are constantly emerging at the Commission while older ones are being downplayed. We can presently identify several such regulatory trends at the FTC.

DEEMPHASIS OF REGULATORY ACTIONS AGAINST
COMPARATIVE PRICE ADVERTISING AND PHONY MOCK-UPS

Writing in the *Harvard Law Review*, Robert Pitofsky, former Director of the FTC's Bureau of Consumer Protection, reveals that during the early 1970's the Commission reduced greatly the number of complaints filed against advertisers for deceptive price claims and misleading mock-ups, favorite targets of regulatory action in the 1950's and 60's. At the same time the Commission refocused its resources to challenge product quality claims—e.g., "10% longer tire wear"—where these claims were potentially deceptive.

In part the Commission changed its attitude toward price claims such as "lowest price in town" and "10% off list" because of the ease with which consumers can check the truthfulness of these claims. Also, the Commission came to view these claims as tools in enabling discounters and others to penetrate a concentrated market without incurring the cost of having to check every other price in the market area before making price claims. As long as consumers are truthfully informed as to the actual price of a product, the Commission presently recognizes that they can make intelligent purchasing decisions.

The reasons behind the reduction of regulatory activity against phony mock-ups are twofold. First, most advertisers currently identify mock-ups as such in advertising which requires their use, thereby negating any possible deception. Second, even where undisclosed, most mock-ups are used accurately to represent real qualities of a product which simply do not film well for television. The consumer is uninjured by this "deception." In any event the FTC has virtually abandoned its attack against the use of mock-ups.

EMPHASIS ON RULE-MAKING AND DISCLOSURE

One of the big steps taken by the FTC in recent years toward upgrading its regulatory efficiency has been its emphasis on formulating Trade Regulation Rules. These published rules identify practices which the Commission will consider violations of Section 5 of the FTC Act. Trade Rules differ from Industry Guides, also promulgated by the Commission, in that violating the former incurs the $10,000 per day fine, but violating the latter does not.

The increased regulatory efficiency of the Trade Rules derives from the fact that they usually apply across-the-board to an entire industry. Under a case-by-case approach to unfair or deceptive advertising practices, the Commission may have to spend several years prosecuting an advertiser for some challenged practice only to find at the conclusion of the successful prosecution that it is also necessary to bring individual cases against each of the advertiser's competitors—all of whom engage in the same practice. This case-by-case approach is not only time consuming and expensive but also may injure competitively the advertiser who is ordered to desist from a challenged practice while competitors continue to engage in the practice. Issuing a Trade Rule is more equitable. It applies to all competitors equally and simultaneously, and it threatens a stiff fine to any who violate it.

Many of the rules promulgated in the last several years force advertisers to disclose various categories of information to consumers. These rules have required notice of octane ratings on gasoline, mileage per gallon for new cars, care labeling instructions on clothes, and average durability of light bulbs. Other rules establish standards for advertising claims, e.g., the minimum mandatory gold content of a product advertised as "gold." Still other rules require warnings be given prospective purchasers, e.g., of the potential side effects of over-the-counter antacids. All of the rules are designed to increase the flow of useful product information to consumers, enabling them to make intelligent purchases.

UNFAIRNESS AS A SEPARATE BASIS FOR REGULATION

Although the Wheeler-Lea Amendment authorizes the FTC to regulate "unfair" as well as "deceptive" trade practices, until recently there has been little concern about "unfair" advertising. Almost all "unfairness" cases prior to 1970 dealt with practices other than advertising (use of scare tactics to induce purchase of furnaces, use of lottery devices in marketing of products, use of threats of law suit to induce purchase of unordered merchandise, use of contract clauses forcing consumers to sue sellers in out-of-state courts). These early cases could likely have been brought as "unfair" to competitors even without the unfair-trade-practices-to-consumers language of the Wheeler-Lea Amendment.

However, in 1972 the Supreme Court strongly affirmed the FTC's authority to declare practices as unfair in their effects on consumers without regard to their effects on competition. The Court in *FTC* v. *Sperry and Hutchinson* compared the Commission to a "court of equity" which must consider "public values" in determining unfair trade practices. While the *S&H* case did not deal with advertising, it is applicable to the broader term *trade practices* which includes advertising. Thus the stage was set for the extension of the unfairness doctrine as a separate basis (beyond deception) for advertising regulation.

This extension came also in 1972 with the Commission's trade regulation case *Pfizer, Inc.* In *Pfizer* the full five member Commission unanimously challenged the claim that the sun lotion "Unburn" contained a secret ingredient that anesthetizes the skin nerves and ruled it "unfair" to make affirmative product claims without their being backed by adequate prior substantiation—even if the claims turned out to be truthful. One impact of this case has been to force advertisers to ensure that advertising claims have been substantiated prior to being made. The FTC has followed its *Pfizer* decision with a substantiation program requiring various sellers on an industry-wide basis to produce data in support of recent advertising claims.

In spite of the *S&H* and *Pfizer* cases, the FTC has moved slowly in developing unfairness as a new basis for advertising regulation. There is some evidence that the FTC considers it unfair for an advertiser to fail to disclose pertinent information in certain situations. Several formal complaints have asserted that it is unfair for vocational school advertisements to fail to disclose the percentage of graduates who obtain jobs. It has also been suggested that another potential use of the unfairness concept would be to protect audiences who possess special vulnerablilities from advertising aimed at exploiting them. Even if non-deceptive such advertisements might be unfair if aimed at pregnant women, children, the old, the poor, etc.

Use of the electronic media (TV and radio) in advertising could bring about an extension of the unfairness doctrine. While the Commission has not yet taken formal steps in this direction, there is growing indication that individual staff members within the FTC are aware that electronic advertising may affect people differently than print advertising. Television and radio advertising are more intrusive and less easy to avoid than print advertising, and there is some thought that the aural and visual immediacy of electronic advertising is used more to induce emotional predispositions toward advertised products than to provide substantive information about intrinsic product characteristics. In

1977 the Director of the FTC's Bureau of Consumer Protection called for regulation of advertising's "total sensory impact," warning that electronic commercialism must be considered differently from other advertising forms for both regulatory and First Amendment purposes.

NEW FTC REMEDIES AND PENALTIES

The FTC has always possessed the power to design flexible remedies for use in cases involving unfair or deceptive advertising. Until recently, though, the usual remedies were the straight cease-and-desist and the consent order under which the advertiser was "to go and sin no more." The only penalty was a $5,000 per day fine arising *after* a formal order had been violated. Since 1970, however, there have been several new remedies worthy of note, which have been developed either under existing Commission powers or under new authority granted by Congress.

In 1974 Congress passed the Federal Trade Commission Improvement Act, which granted several new remedies to the FTC. The Act empowered the Commission to seek injunctions from the Federal District Court to restrain the continuance of advertising campaigns under certain circumstances while the Commission is determining whether or not the campaign violates Section 5. Previously, advertisers were usually able to delay through legal maneuvering the imposition of a cease-and-desist order until after the advertising campaign had run its course. The new Act also enabled the FTC to force advertisers to compensate consumers injured by a Section 5 violation, and it increased the penalty for violating a Commission Trade Rule or order to $10,000 per day. The Act also affirmed the Commission's authority to issue Trade Rules, an authority which had been challenged in federal court by advertisers.

Developed by the commission under its existing powers, one of the most important new remedies is that of "corrective advertising," first initiated in 1970. In the words of the Commission, its new remedy is to be used in the following situation:

> If a deceptive advertisement has played a substantial role in creating or reinforcing in the public's mind a false and material belief which lives on after the advertising ceases, there is clear and continuing injury to competition and to the consuming public as consumers continue to make purchasing decisions based on the false belief. Since this injury cannot be averted by merely requiring respondent to cease disseminating the advertisement, we may appropriately order respondent to take affirmative action designed to terminate the otherwise continuing ill effects of the advertisement.

Usually, corrective advertising forces an advertiser to spend a designated amount of money to advertise the product in such a way as to correct the previous misimpression. In 1978, for example, the STP company agreed to an FTC consent order which imposed on STP a $500,000 penalty. The consent order also required STP to mount a $200,000 advertising campaign in which STP would admit it had relied on deceptive research in claiming that STP Oil Treatment reduced highway oil consumption by 20%.

As of this writing, advertisers are still challenging in the federal courts the power of the FTC to impose corrective advertising. In the most recent case the U.S. Court of Appeals upheld the Commission's authority to impose such advertising.

REGULATORY USE OF SOCIAL SCIENCE RESEARCH

One of the most interesting trends to marketing researchers is the FTC's increasing use of social science research techniques to determine what particular advertisements mean to consumers. A recent article in the *Journal of Marketing* claimed that the Commission uses consumer surveys in as many as half of its currently litigated cases to establish consumer beliefs arising from advertising. From the lawyer's point of view, however, several legal considerations must qualify the enthusiasm for such research.

First, the questionnaires and surveys constructed through social science research techniques are still imprecise, Variously constructed surveys yield dissimilar results. From a legal viewpoint it may be best for the FTC to avoid challenges as to the validity of such survey results by relying on its own virtually unchallengeable power to interpret the meaning of an advertisement for a "tendency or capacity" to violate Section 5.

Second, the use of surveying methods raises legal evidentiary issues concerning the adequacy of sampling and the rights of defendants to cross-examine the consumers who make up the survey or to have discovery against them. A full consideration of these issues would substantially impede litigation. In any event, the Commission is free to disregard survey results if it finds them unpersuasive since the weighing of conflicting evidence is within the Commission's sole discretion.

FIRST AMENDMENT LIMITATIONS ON ADVERTISING REGULATION

In 1942 the Supreme Court declared that the First Amendment's freedom of speech guarantees did not apply to commercial speech. Thirty-three years later the Court reversed itself, holding that commercial as well as political and religious expression is embraced by the First Amendment. In cases involving state and local prohibitions against advertisements for abortions, prescription drugs, professional services, and house sales, the Court explored and interpreted the First Amendment ramifications of advertising.

The cases in aggregate require that challenges to advertising regulation be resolved by "assessing the First Amendment interest at stake and weighing it against the public interest allegedly served by the regulation." Focusing on advertising as a means for communicating ideas and information, the cases justify First Amendment protection of advertising as it functions to lead citizens toward intelligent, informed economic decisions. It is important for students to grasp, however, that constitutional protections for commercial speech do not mean that no regulation is justified or permitted. In dicta the Court has intimated that the FTC's regulation of advertising under Section 5 could continue by pointing out that fraudulent, false, and misleading advertising inhibits efficient, economic decision making. Thus, commercial speech has not yet been accorded the same constitutional status as political and religious speech, which is usually protected even when "false."

The importance of the Court's recent decision to FTC advertising regulation lies in possible constitutional challenges to Commission actions which define new categories of "unfair" advertisements and create new remedies such as corrective advertising. In each instance advertisers can be expected to challenge vigorously these new developments on First Amendment grounds. The outer limits of constitutional protection for commercial expression are still far from being fixed.

CONCLUSION

Advertising plays an important role in facilitating intelligent, economic decisions in our private enterprise system. In this chapter we have examined the regulation of advertising by its most influential legal critic—the Federal Trade Commission. The Commission's early history, the Wheeler-Lea Amendment, some traditional categories of deceptive advertising, the procedural course of a Commission litigation, recent trends in FTC advertising regulation, and the implications of First Amendment protection for commercial expression are discussed. A grasp of these materials should provide students with a substantial basis for further consideration of the regulation of advertising.

12

Unfair Competition

John R. Allison*

One of the most basic precepts in the American economic and legal systems is that of *competition*. It is generally felt that if free market forces are allowed to operate without artificial hindrances, competition will bring about the most efficient use and allocation of resources. And economically efficient utilization of capital and labor brings prices to a lower level, and service and innovation to a higher level, than would occur in the absence of viable competition. Our antitrust laws are, of course, aimed at fostering competition by removing from the machinery of free enterprise such artificial impediments as price fixing or territorial divisions among competitors or the possession of monopoly power by a single firm.

Competition in the marketplace can be rigorous, sometimes even cutthroat. As we have observed, competition is generally encouraged by the law, regardless of its rigors or its effect on weaker or less efficient firms. There is a line, however, beyond which competition passes from the *rigorous* to the *unfair*. The laws prohibiting "unfair competition" (which are part of the law of torts) have as their underlying premise the idea that in certain situations the basic policy in favor of competition is outweighed by the harm that results from competitive practices which cross traditional boundaries of reasonable and ethical business behavior.

This chapter will explore the following areas of the law of unfair competition: (1) trade disparagement; (2) false representations about one's own product; (3) trademark infringement; and (4) misappropriation of trade secrets. Although some federal law is involved it should be noted that it is the "private law" of unfair competition, enforced in lawsuits by private parties, that is dealt with in this chapter. Thus, the enforcement activities of the Federal Trade Commission with respect to false advertising and other species of unfair competition are beyond the scope of this discussion.

---

*University of Texas at Austin.

TRADE DISPARAGEMENT

The tort of trade disparagement (or "trade libel") is committed when one party makes false statements of fact relating to the quality of another's (usually a competitor's) goods or services. The following case discusses this aspect of the law of unfair competition and provides an apt illustration of its application.

■ ■ ■

Testing Systems, Inc. v. Magnaflux Corp.
U.S. District Court for the
Eastern District of Pennsylvania
251 F. Supp. 286 (1966)

JOHN W. LORD, Jr. District Judge.

This is an action for trade libel or disparagement of property. Jurisdiction is predicated on diversity of citizenship and the requisite amount in controversy. The matter is now before this Court on the defendant's motion to dismiss for failure to state a claim upon which relief can be granted.

Essentially the facts are these. Both plaintiff, Testing Systems, Inc., and the defendant, Magnaflux Corp., are engaged in the manufacture and sale of equipment, devices and systems, including chemical products, for use in the non-destructive testing of commercial and industrial materials. The allegedly actionable statements concern similar chemical products of the parties; that of the plaintiff being known as "Flaw Finder", and that of the defendant identified as "Spotcheck". The complaint contains allegations that both written and oral statements disparaging plaintiff's product were circulated by the defendant's agents to plaintiff's current and prospective customers. Specifically, in the former category, it is alleged that the defendant did on or about May 6, 1965, through its agents, publish an allegedly false report to the effect that the United States Government had tested plaintiff's product, and found it to be only about 40% as effective as that of the defendant.

It appears further from the complaint that on or about May 23, 1965, while in attendance at a manufacturer's convention in Philadelphia, defendant's agent, in the presence of plaintiff's current and prospective customers, "did in a loud voice state that * * * [plaintiff's] * * * stuff is no good," and that "the government is throwing them out."

For the purposes of this motion, defendant admits the truth of the allegations, but asserts that the action must nevertheless be dismissed because the defendant did no more than make an unfavorable comparison of plaintiff's product with its own * * * .

It would serve no useful purpose to dwell at length on the issue of unfavorable comparison. Suffice it to say, as the defendant properly points out, that a statement which takes the form of an unfavorable comparison of products, or which "puffs" or exaggerates the quality of one's own product is not ordinarily actionable. This has long been the rule in England, where the action originated, and is now well established in the vast majority of United States jurisdictions.

However, this Court is not convinced by the defendant's arguments that his comments amounted to mere unfavorable comparison. The modern history of the doctrine of unfavorable comparison and its permissible use in the conduct of business traces its origin to the leading English case of *White v. Mellin*, (1895) A.C. 154. There the defendant had advertised his product as being far more healthful than plaintiff's. In refusing relief the Court established the precedent that irrespective of their truth or falsity, statements by one competitior which compare his product with that of another are not actionable.

It does not follow from this, however, that every trade disparagement is protectible under the guise of unfavorable comparison merely because the perpetrator was canny enough to mention not only the product of his competitor but also his own. The decision in *White v. Mellin*, supra, was founded on the near impossibility of ascertaining the truth or falsity of general allegations respecting the superiority of one product over another. To decide otherwise, explained Lord Herschell, would turn the courts "into a machinery for advertising rival productions by obtaining a judicial determination [as to] which of the two was better." 2 Callman, Unfair Competition and Trademarks, § 41.2 (2 ed. 1950). One is expected to believe in the superiority of his wares, and he may properly declare his belief to interested parties.

* * * The fine line that separates healthy competitive effort from underhanded business tactics is frequently difficult to determine. Apart from the tradesman's right of free speech, which must be vigorously safeguarded, the public has a genuine interest in learning the relative merits of particular products, however that may come about. To advance these interests the law of the market place gives the competitor a wide berth in the conduct of his business. As Mr. Justice Maxey of the Pennsylvania Supreme Court said in 1932,

> "[H]e may send out circulars, or give information verbally, to customers of other men, knowing they are bound by contract for a definite term, although acting upon the expectation and with the purpose of getting the trade of such persons for himself.

> "[H]e may use any mode of persuasion with such a customer * * * which appeals to his self-interest, reason, or even his prejudices.

> "[H]e may descant upon the extent of his rival's facilities compared with his own, his rival's means, his insolvency, if it be a fact, and the benefits which will result to the customer in the future from coming to the solicitor rather than remaining where he is.

> * * * [T]he law of competition' * * * takes little note of the ordinary rules of good neighborhood or abstract morality."

Nonetheless, there is an outer perimeter to permissible conduct. The tradesman must be assured that his competitors will not be suffered to engage in conduct which falls below the minimum standard of fair dealing. "[I]t is no answer that they can defend themselves by also resorting to disparagement. A self-respecting business man will not voluntarily adopt, and should not be driven to adopt, a selling method which he regards as undignified, unfair, and repulsive. A competitor should not, by pursuing an unethical practice force his rival to choose between its adoption and the loss of his trade." (Wolfe, Unfair Competition, 47 Yale L.J. 1304, 1334-35 (1938).)

The defendant's comments in the case presently before this Court do not entitle him to the protection accorded to "unfavorable comparison." There is a readily observable difference between saying that one's product is, in general, better than another's (though even this is subject to serious objection, see Callman, supra, § 41.2) and asserting, as here, that such other's is only 40% as effective as one's own. The former, arguably, merely expresses an opinion, the truth or falsity of which is difficult or impossible of ascertainment. The latter, however, is an assertion of fact, not subject to the same frailties of proof, implying that the party making the statement is fortified with the substantive facts necessary to make it. This distinction has never been seriously questioned. The defendant in this case admittedly circulated to plaintiff's present and prospective customers false statements to the effect that the government had tested both products and found the defendant's to be 60% more effective than the plaintiff's. This is not the sort of "comparison" that courts will protect.

Apart from this, there is at least one additional factor which withdraws the defendant's comments from the category of unfavorable comparison. Not content with making the admittedly false statements and allowing them to be evaluated independently of all extraneous influence, the defendant here gave added authenticity to its assertions by invoking the reputation of a third party, the United States Government. It is unnecessary to speculate on the additional force the defendant's remarks must have had when coupled with the purported approval of so highly credible a source. This, of course, is to say nothing of the statements to the effect that the plaintiff had been "thrown out," which by no stretch of the imagination could be termed mere comparison.

For all of the above reasons, it is the judgment of this Court that the defendant's remarks are actionable. [That is, the plaintiff's complaint does allege facts which, if proved, will establish a claim against defendant.] * * *

■ ■ ■

FALSE REPRESENTATIONS ABOUT ONE'S OWN PRODUCT

We saw in the previous section that a party can be held liable for making false statements of fact about his competitor's goods or services. In this section we will see that one can also be liable for making false representations about *his own* goods or services. In either case, the misrepresentations must relate to facts, rather than being mere expressions of opinion or general "sales talk." The primary legal basis of liability for misrepresentations about one's own products is a federal statute, section 43(a) of the Lanham Act. The following case illustrates one of the innumerable types of situations to which this statute applies.

■ ■ ■

CBS, Inc. v. Gusto Records, Inc.
U.S. District Court for the
Middle District of Tennessee
403 F. Supp. 447 (1974)

MORTON, District Judge.

This is an action by plaintiffs CBS, Inc. and Charles Allen Rich (professionally known as Charlie Rich) against Gusto Records, Inc. Plaintiffs seek a preliminary injunction against defendant corporation pursuant to Rule 65 of the Federal Rules of Civil Procedure, pending a trial of their cause against defendant.

Plaintiffs would have this court issue a preliminary injunction enjoining the defendant, Gusto Records, Inc., its officers, agents, servants and employees and all persons acting in concert with it, from manufacturing, advertising, distributing, selling, or offering for sale, recordings, whether phonograph record albums or tape recordings, entitled "Charlie Rich—The Silver Fox," or bearing a current likeness of the plaintiff Rich. Plaintiffs allege that such an injunction will prevent irreparable injury to them.

Plaintiffs' pending cause of action is brought pursuant to Section 43(a) of the Lanham Act * * * . In their complaint, plaintiffs charge defendant Gusto Records, Inc. with unauthorized, unfair and deceptive practices in connection with the manufacture, distribution and sale of a record album entitled "Charlie Rich—The Silver Fox."

Plaintiff Rich is currently under contract to CBS, Inc., which is planning to release a record album which is also entitled "Charlie Rich—The Silver Fox." Plaintiffs allege that defendant's record will interfere with the sales of the CBS album, and that the misrepresentations of the defendant as to the contents of the Gusto album will irreparably injure Mr. Rich's reputation and popularity as a recording star.

At the outset, this court must determine whether the Gusto album, "Charlie Rich—The Silver Fox," which is marketed under the "Power Pak" label, is packaged in such a way as to be violative of Section 43(a) of the Lanham Act * * *. [This section] provides in part:

"(a) Any person who shall affix, apply, or annex, or use in connection with any goods or services, or any container or containers for goods . . . any false description or representation, including words or other symbols tending falsely to describe or represent the same, and shall cause such goods or services to enter into commerce . . . shall be liable to a civil action . . . by any person who believes that he is or is likely to be damaged by the use of any such false description or misrepresentation."

Cases have held that this section of the Lanhan Act creates a federal statutory tort *sui generis*, and that it is not necessary for the plaintiff to show that misrepresentation was willful or intentional. In seeking injunctive relief, it is not necessary that plaintiff show that the public has actually been deceived; the likelihood of deception and confusion is sufficient.

The question before this court, then, is whether the Gusto album "Charlie Rich—The Silver Fox" is packaged in such a way that there is a liklihood that the public will be misled and confused as to its true contents. This court finds the album cover to be misleading and deceptive, in violation of Section 43(a) of the Lanham Act.

The recordings on the Gusto "Power Pak" album, "Charlie Rich—The Silver Fox" are primarily songs which were recorded by Mr. Rich some ten to fifteen years ago, prior to his current fame and success. Mr. Rich's singing style at that time was considerably different from his style of today, and technology in the industry was not as advanced as it is today. The songs in question were originally recorded monaurally; defendant has "overdubbed" the originals in order to create a stereo effect. There is some dispute as to whether the album qualifies as a true stereo album, although it is labeled "Stereo" on the back of the jacket cover. Prominently displayed on the front cover is a current picture of Mr. Rich, which creates the impression that the recordings have been made recently. This impression is strengthened by the use of the nickname "The Silver Fox" in conjunction with Mr. Rich, the nickname being of fairly recent origin. The names of the songs contained in the album are also listed on the front cover, but no recording date is given. The only date given is that on the back cover of the jacket, and it is 1974.

Totally absent from either side of the cover is any information which would inform the consumer that the recordings contained in the album were recorded over a decade ago. Even if the consumer were an unusually informed country music fan and knew when the songs were originally recorded by Mr. Rich, he would have no way of knowing that they had not been re-recorded by the now successful Mr. Rich, in keeping with his current style. In fact, the impression conveyed is to the contrary. The record albums are sealed, and an expert witness testified at the hearing that a customer has no way of hearing the record prior to purchase in the usual retail situation.

For the foregoing reasons, this court can only conclude that the packaging tends to falsely describe the contents of the record album, in violation of Section 43(a) of the Lanham Act.

We turn now to the question of irreparable damages, a prerequisite for injunctive relief. Defendant, Gusto Records, Inc. is attempting to market at least 50,000 copies of the "Power Pak" album, "Charlie Rich—The Silver Fox." If these records are allowed to go on the market in their current jacket covers, there is little doubt that many consumers would be disappointed when they became aware of the contents of the album. It is highly possible that they might attribute the deception to Charlie Rich himself, or that they might think that Mr. Rich had changed his style of singing, if they were not aware that the recordings were made over a decade ago. The damage to Mr. Rich's reputation and popularity might well be considerable and irreparable.

Despite these findings, this court has serious reservations about granting the blanket injunction requested by the plaintiffs. The resulting financial harm to Gusto Records, Inc. would be considerable, and the exact damages difficult to ascertain, should the defendant prevail at the trial on the merits. Defendant, as a gesture of good faith and without admission of any liability, has offered to affix a decal to each of the albums in question, clarifying the contents of the album. The court has given this suggestion considerable thought, and has come to the conclusion that such an accurate statement of the album's contents, if affixed in a prominent location on the album jacket, would alleviate any irreparable harm which might be caused to plaintiffs by defendant's violation of Section 43(a) of the Lanham Act. The court considers the wording "Early Monaural Recording of Charlie Rich, Adapted for Stereo" to be a reasonably accurate statement of the album's contents. A bright orange decal containing such language, printed in black ink, and with dimensions of at least three and one-half inches by one and one-half inches, will be affixed to each album cover directly over the photograph of Mr. Rich. * * *

■ ■ ■

TRADEMARK INFRINGEMENT

The Lanham Act not only prohibits false representations about one's products, as we have already seen, but this federal statute also provides for registration and protection of trademarks. Indeed, most of the Lanham Act's provisions are concerned with trademarks.

A trademark is defined in section 45 as "any word, name, symbol or device or any combination thereof adopted or used by a manufacturer or merchant to identify his goods and distinguish them from those manufactured or sold by others." This section also defines a "service mark" (used in connection with the sale of services rather than goods) in a similar way. The same rules of law apply to both.

Simply registering a trademark with the U.S. Patent Office does not give the registrant exclusive rights in the mark. In American trademark law, *use* of the mark in connection with the sale of goods or services is essential for the mark to be protected. In fact, the U.S. Patent Office will not permit registration unless there is evidence that the mark has been used in interstate commerce. And if a formerly valid trademark is later *abandoned*, as evidenced by a cessation of use for a substantial period of time, the owner of the mark loses the exclusive right to it. The requirement of use is contrary to the law of most other countries, where registration with the appropriate government agency is all that is required.

The following case is a fairly typical example of trademark litigation and contains an illuminating discussion of several basic principles of trademark law.

■ ■ ■

Safeway Stores, Inc. v. Stephens
U.S. District Court for the
Western District of Louisiana
281 F. Supp. 517 (1967)

BEN C. DAWKINS, Jr., Chief Judge.

This is a suit for infringement of the service mark and trade-mark "Safeway," owned by petitioner and registered by it in the United States Patent Office, and to stop unfair competition. The relief sought is for permanent injunction against respondent who is engaged in business in Natchitoches, Louisiana.

* * *

Safeway Stores, Incorporated is organized under the laws of Maryland and has been authorized continuously to transact business in Louisiana since January, 1943. Petitioner and its predecessors in interest have continuously used "Safeway" as the dominant part of their corporate name on a national basis since 1925, and petitioner has used "Safeway" both as a trade name and as a trade-mark on a national basis since 1941. The nature of Safeway's business is that of a food or grocery retailer and at the present time Safeway is the second largest retailer of its kind in the United States.

* * *

That petitioner owns valid and existing service mark and trade-mark registrations issued by the United States Patent Office is undisputed. The mark and name of "Safeway" is and has been used in Louisiana since 1947, and has been registered with the Secretary of State since that time. This trade name and service mark have at all times been prominently displayed on all of petitioner's stores and vehicles which number in the thousands. Operations of Safeway Stores, Incorporated extend to the State of Mississippi and all States west of the Mississippi River except Minnesota, Wisconsin and North Dakota. Safeway's stock is traded on several of the national exchanges, including the New York Stock Exchange, and its annual cost of advertising exceeds Twenty Million Dollars ($20,000,000).

Petitioner's retail operations in Louisiana include: four stores in Monroe and West Monroe; a recently opened store in Bastrop; plans for additional stores in the Monroe area and also in Ruston which is some 80 miles from Natchitoches. Although petitioner has no outlet in Natchitoches, Louisiana, the location of respondent's store, petitioner's advertisements, especially through television, reach residents of Natchitoches daily.

Respondent Stephens is the sole proprietor of the concern known as "Save-Way Food Center & Save-Way Dairy Bar" and has been doing business under that name for fourteen years. According to respondent, the name "Save-Way" was selected in a contest specifically designed to choose a name for the business, with $25.00 being awarded for the winning suggestion. At the time of the contest in 1952, respondent knew of the existence of Safeway Stores, Incorporated, and knew of their status as a leading national food company. Respondent also admitted that there had been occasional inquiries by people whether the business owned and operated by him had any connection with Safeway Stores, Incorporated.

Respondent has never applied for a trade or sevice mark for the name now used in his business, and is not authorized to do business in Louisiana under that name at this time. In some advertisements, respondent has used an "S" similar to that registered to petitioner. In the fourteen years of operation including the year 1965, respondent's business has shown remarkable growth from gross sales of some $123,000 in 1952, to almost $925,000 in 1965. Advertising costs for respondent in 1965 totaled around $6,000, 95% of which was spent in the local newspaper, *The Natchitoches Times*. It has been stipulated that parties to this suit are engaged in the identical business, i.e., the retail grocery business.

Petitioner alleges that it first learned of respondent's use of the name "Save-Way" in March, 1964, when Safeway Stores, Incorporated was served through its agent for service of process in an action originally entitled "Walter M. Clary and Ruby Woodel Clary v. Wesley Stephens d/b/a Safeway Food Store, et al." The suit was against Stephens, *Safeway Stores* and *Safeway's* insurer, the Travelers' Insurance Company. At a later date, counsel for the Clarys, finding that *Safeway* was in no way connected with respondent Stephens or his operation of *Save-Way*, dismissed the action against petitioner and its insurer. On or about September 20, 1964, petitioner demanded that respondent terminate its use of the term "Save-Way" or variations confusingly similar to "Safeway". These facts gave rise to the present litigation.

In an action for trade-mark infringement, it has often been repeated that the controlling issue is whether the alleged infringer's use of a particular mark "is likely to cause confusion, or to cause mistake, or to deceive, * * *." Furthermore, direct competition between the products marketed is not a prerequisite to protective relief. The remedies of the owner of a registered trade-mark are not limited to the goods specified in the certificate, but extend to any goods on which the use of an infringing mark is "likely to cause confusion * * *." Confusion or the likelihood of confusion, not competition, is the real test of trade-mark infringement. Whether direct competition exists is but one of the elements to be considered in determining that there is a likelihood of confusion. Regardless of whether a word or words adopted and used as a trade-mark or trade name could be characterized as geographical in nature, where such words have acquired a "secondary meaning," the courts will afford equitable protection to the party whose use of the word has created the secondary meaning. It deserves protection when, because of association with a particular product or firm over a period of time, the word has come to stand in the mind of the public as a name or identification for that product or firm. Protection is warranted on what it has come to signify regardless of any original weakness, actual or supposed. The fact that the alleged infringer is in good faith and has no actual intention to mislead the public is not a defense. It is enough that such result is "probable." It has been held that trade-mark infringement is recognized to be an aspect of the broader field of unfair competition. The burden is upon the latecomer to avoid confusion, mistake or deception and if doubt exists, it must be resolved against him.

Relying on the pertinent sections of the Lanham Act, petitioner has introduced ample evidence to show that it is entitled to injunctive relief based on trade-mark infringement and unfair competition because of respondent's adoption and use, without consent, of a trade name which is deceptively similar to petitioner's registered service mark and trade-mark namely "Safeway." No authority is needed to support the proposition that the term "Save-Way" used by respondent is so alike in sound and appearance to petitioner's mark and name, "Safeway," as to cause and to be likely to cause confusion or mistake, or to deceive purchasers, when applied in connection with the sale of grocery products. The two terms are almost indistinguishable when heard over the news media or even printed in the newspaper.

Respondent has admitted that several inquiries were made to him concerning the connection between his business and that of petitioner. Affidavits filed in the record reveal additional instances of confusion on the part of people who have moved to Natchitoches from communities where Safeway stores were actually located. Further confusion is vividly illustrated in the damage suit filed against petitioner in the mistaken belief that petitioner and respondent were in fact connected in the grocery business.

Besides the uncontroverted instances of actual confusion mentioned above, a comparison of pictures of stores of the two parties shows that respondent uses block-type lettering that is extremely similar to that long in use by petitioner. Exhibits introduced by petitioner graphically illustrate that advertisements in the local newspaper by respondent included an insigne similar to that registered to petitioner. Enhancing the "likelihood of confusion" is the fact that the parties are engaged in the identical business of selling groceries at retail. Because petitioner does not actually have a retail store located in Natchitoches, the Court now considers whether petitioner's trade name and mark have taken on what is commonly known as a "secondary meaning" within a geographic region.

There is little or no doubt that the term "Safeway" and the retail grocery business have become identified with petitioner's business in the public mind. Petitioner has expended considerable sums in the advertising field on a national basis and this has reached the region and town in question. The fact that Safeway does not have a store in Natchitoches does not preclude granting the relief prayed for here because prior cases have held that it is of no essence that the parties are not actually in geographic competition. Moreover, in the instant case there is a possibility of geographic competition because Natchitoches is in the area generally known as the "Ark-La-Tex" where numerous Safeway stores are located. An established trade name is entitled to protection not only in the area in which it already renders service or sells goods, but also to areas in which its trade reasonably may be expected to expand.

Based upon the evidence presented and the principles of law applicable to this case, we find that respondent, a latecomer, has deliberately failed to avoid confusion, mistake or deception in this situation. The evidence is overwhelmingly in favor of petitioner's position. No evidence has been presented by respondent and no brief has been filed on his behalf.

We therefore hold that an injunction should be issued restraining respondent, Wesley Stephens, d/b/a/ Save-Way Food Center and Save-Way Dairy Bar, from use of the name Save-Way or any similar name or symbol which in any way might tend to, or be likely to, cause confusion, mistake or tend to deceive. Respondent is granted sixty days after receiving notice of the injunction to be issued herein within which to report in writing under oath the manner and form in which he has complied with our order.

Because petitioner claims attorney's fees in the amount of $10,000, the case will be held open on this issue alone and petitioner shall have sixty days from service of the judgment to be issued pursuant to this decision to present evidence in support of its claim to attorney's fees in a reasonable amount. * * *

■ ■ ■

MISAPPROPRIATION OF TRADE SECRETS

The following case not only outlines the basic principles of trade secret and patent law, but it also resolves a longstanding question as to the constitutional validity of the law of trade secrets.

■ ■ ■

Kewanee Oil Co. v. Bicron Corporation
Supreme Court of the United States
416 U.S. 470 (1974)

[*Harshaw Chemical Co., a division of Kewanee Oil Co., petitioner, is a leading manufacturer of a type of synthetic crystal which is useful in the detection of ionizing radiation. In 1949 Harshaw commenced research into the growth of this type crystal and was able to produce one less than two inches in diameter. By 1966, as the result of expenditures in excess of $1 million, Harshaw was able to grow a 17-inch crystal, something no one else had done previously. Harshaw had developed many processes, procedures, and manufacturing techniques in the purification of raw materials and the growth and encapsulation of the crystals which enabled it to accomplish this feat. Some of these processes Harshaw considers to be trade secrets. Several former employees of Harshaw formed Bicron, respondent, in August 1969 to compete with Harshaw in the production of the crystals; by April 1970 Bicron had grown a 17-inch crystal. Petitioner filed suit, seeking an injunction and damages for the alleged misappropriation of trade secrets. The federal district court, applying Ohio trade secret law, granted a permanent injunction against respondent and its employees which prohibited disclosure or use of 20 of the 40 claimed trade secrets until such time as the trade secrets had been released to the public, had otherwise become available to the public, or had been obtained by respondents from sources having the legal right to convey the information. The court of appeals reversed the district court, holding Ohio's trade secret law to be in conflict with the patent laws of the United States. Petitioners then asked the U.S. Supreme Court to review the case; the Court consented by granting a writ of certiorari.*]

Mr. Chief Justice Burger delivered the opinion of the Court. * * *

Ohio has adopted the widely relied-upon definition of a trade secret found at Restatement of Torts § 757 * * *,

"[a] trade secret may consist of any formula, pattern, device or compilation of information which is used in one's business, and which gives him an opportunity to obtain an advantage over competitors who do not know or use it. It may be a formula for a chemical compound, a process of manufacturing, treating or preserving materials, a pattern for a machine or other devise, or a list of customers."

The subject of a trade secret must be secret, and must not be of public knowledge or of a general knowledge in the trade or business. This necessary element of secrecy is not lost, however, if the holder of the trade secret reveals the trade secret to another "in confidence, and under an implied obligation not to use or disclose it." These others may include those of the holder's "employees to whom it is necessary to confide it, in order to apply it to the uses for which it is intended." Often the recipient of confidential knowledge of the subject of a trade secret is a licensee of its holder. The protection accorded the trade secret holder is against the disclosure or unauthorized use of the trade secret by those to whom the secret has been confided under the express or implied restriction of nondisclosure or nonuse. The law also protects the holder of a trade secret against disclosure or use when the knowledge is gained, not by the owner's volition, but by some "improper means," Restatement of Torts § 757(a), which may include theft, wiretapping, or even aerial reconnaissance. A trade secret law, however, does not offer protection against discovery by fair and honest means, such as by independent invention, accidental disclosure, or by so-called reverse engineering, that is by starting with the known product and working backward to divine the process which aided in its development or manufacture.

Novelty, in the patent law sense, is not required for a trade secret. "Quite clearly discovery is something less than invention." However, some novelty will be required if merely because that which does not possess novelty is usually known; secrecy, in the context of trade secrets, thus implies at least minimal novelty.

The subject matter of a patent is limited to a "process, machine, manufacture, or composition of matter, or. . . improvement thereof," 35 U.S.C. § 101, which fulfills the three conditions of novelty and utility as articulated and defined in 35 U.S.C. §§ 101 and 102, and nonobviousness, as set out in 35 U.S.C. § 103. If an invention meets the rigorous statutory tests for the issuance of a patent, the patent is granted, for a period of 17 years, giving what has been described as the "right of exclusion." This protection goes not only to copying the subject matter, * * * but also to independent creation.

The first issue we deal with is whether the States are forbidden to act at all in the area of protection of the kinds of intellectual property which may make up the subject matter of trade secrets.

Article I, § 8, cl. 8, of the Constitution grants to the Congress the power.

"[T]o promote the Progress of Science and useful Arts, by securing for limited Times to Authors and Inventors the exclusive Right to their respective Writings and Discoveries . . ."

In the 1972 Term, in *Goldstein* v. *California,* 412 U.S. 546 (1973), we held that the cl. 8 grant of power to Congress was not exclusive and that, at least in the case of writings, the States were not prohibited from encouraging and protecting the efforts of those within their borders by appropriate legislation. The States could, therefore, protect against the unauthorized rerecording for sale of performances fixed on records or tapes, even though these performances qualified as "writtings" in the constitutional sense and Congress was empowered to legislate regarding such performances and could pre-empt the area if it chose to do so. This determination was premised on the great diversity of interests in our Nation—the essentially non-uniform character of the appreciation of intellectual achievements in the various States. * * *

Just as the States may exercise regulatory power over writings so may the States regulate with respect to discoveries. States may hold diverse viewpoints in protecting intellectual property relating to invention as they do in protecting the intellectual property relating to the subject matter of copyright. The only limitation on the States is that in regulating the area of patents and copyrights they do not conflict with the operation of the laws in this area passed by Congress, and it is to that more difficult question we now turn.

The question of whether the trade secret law of Ohio is void under the Supremacy Clause involves a consideration of whether that law "stands as an obstacle to the accomplishment and execution of the full purposes and objectives of Congress." We stated in *Sears, Roebuck & Co.* v. *Stiffel Co.,* 376 U.S. 225 (1964), that when state law touches upon the area of federal statutes enacted pursuant to constitutional authority, "it is 'familiar doctrine' that the federal policy 'may not be set at naught, or its benefits denied' by the state law. This is true, of course, even if the state law is enacted in the exercise of otherwise undoubted state power."

The laws which the Court of Appeals in this case held to be in conflict with the Ohio law of trade secrets were the patent laws passed by the Congress in the unchallenged exercise of its clear power under Art. I, § 8, cl. 8, of the Constitution. The patent law does not explicitly endorse or forbid the operation of trade secret law. However, as we have noted, if the scheme of protection developed by Ohio respecting trade secrets "clashes with the objectives of the federal patent laws," then the state law must fall. To determine whether the Ohio law "clashes" with the federal law it is helpful to examine the objectives of both the patent and trade secret laws.

The stated objective of the Constitution in granting the power to Congress to legislate in the area of intellectual property is to "promote the Progress of Science and useful Arts." The patent laws promote this progress by offering a right of exclusion for a limited period as an incentive to inventors to risk the often enormous costs in terms of time, research, and development. The productive effort thereby fostered will have a positive effect on society through the introduction of new products and processes of manufacture into the economy, and the emanations by way of increased employment and better lives for our citizens. In return for the right of exclusion—this "reward for inventions"—the patent laws impose upon the inventor a requirement of disclosure. To insure adequate and full disclosure so that upon the expiration of the 17-year period "the knowledge of the invention enures to the people, who are thus enabled without restriction to practice it and profit by its use," the patent laws require that the patent application shall include a full and clear description of the invention and "of the manner and process of making and using it" so that any person skilled in the art may make and use the invention. When a patent is granted and the information contained in it is circulated to the general public and those especially skilled in the trade, such additions to the general store of knowledge are of such importance to the public weal that the Federal Government is willing to pay the high price of 17 years of exclusive use for its disclosure, which disclosure, it is assumed, will stimulate ideas and the eventual development of further significant advances in the art. The Court has also articulated another policy of the patent law: that which is in the public domain cannot be removed therefrom by action of the States.

"[F]ederal law requires that all ideas in general circulation be dedicated to the common good unless they are protected by a valid patent." Lear, Inc. v. Adkins, 395 U.S., at 668."

The maintenance of standards of commercial ethics and the encouragement of invention are the broadly stated policies behind trade secret law. "The necessity of good faith and honest, fair dealing, is the very life and spirit of the commercial world." In *A.O. Smith Corp. v. Petroleum Iron Works Co.,* 73 F.2d, at 539, the Court emphasized that even though a discovery may not be patentable, that does not

"destroy the value of the discovery to one who makes it, or advantage the competitor who by unfair means, or as the beneficiary of a broken faith, obtains the desired knowledge without himself paying the price in labor, money, or machines expended by the discoverer."

* * * Having now in mind the objectives of both the patent and trade secret law, we turn to an examination of the interaction of these systems of protection of intellectual property—one established by the Congress and the other by a State—to determine whether and under what circumstances the latter might constitute "too great an encroachment on the federal patent system to be tolerated."

As we noted earlier, trade secret law protects items which would not be proper subjects for consideration for patent protection. As in the case of the recordings in *Goldstein v. California,* Congress, with respect to nonpatentable subject matter, "has drawn no balance; rather, it has left the area unattended, and no reason exists why the State should not be free to act."

Since no patent is available for a discovery, however useful, novel, and nonobvious, unless it falls within one of the express categories of patentable subject matter of 35 U.S.C. § 101, the holder of such a discovery would have no reason to apply for a patent whether trade secret protection existed or not. Abolition of trade secret protection would, therefore, not result in increased disclosure to the public of discoveries in the area of nonpatentable subject matter. Also, it is hard to see how the public would be benefited by disclosure of customer lists or advertising campaigns; in fact, keeping such items secret encourages businesses to initiate new and individualized plans of operation, and constructive competition results. This, in turn, leads to a greater variety of business methods than would otherwise be the case if privately developed marketing and other data were passed illicitly among firms involved in the same enterprise.

Congress has spoken in the area of those discoveries which fall within one of the categories of patentable subject matter of 35 U.S.C. § 101 and which are, therefore, of a nature that would be subject to consideration for a patent. Processes, machines, manufactures, compositions of matter and improvements thereof, which meet the tests of utility, novelty, and nonobviousness are entitled to be patented, but those which do not, are not. The question remains whether those items which are proper subjects for consideration for a patent may also have available the alternative protection accorded by trade secret law.

Certainly the patent policy of encouraging invention is not disturbed by the existence of another form of incentive to invention. In this respect the two systems are not and never would be in conflict. Similarly, the policy that matter once in the public domain must remain in the public domain is not incompatible with the existence of trade secret protection. By definition a trade secret has not been placed in the public domain.

The more difficult objective of the patent law to reconcile with trade secret law is that of disclosure, the *quid pro quo* of the right to exclude. * * *

* * * The interest of the public is that the bargain of 17 years of exclusive use in return for disclosure be accepted. If a State, through a system of protection, were to cause a substantial risk that holders of patentable inventions would not seek patents, but rather would rely on the state protection, we would be compelled to hold that such a system could not constitutionally continue to exist. In the case of trade secret law no reasonable risk of deterrence from patent application by those who can reasonably expect to be granted patents exists.

Trade secret law provides far weaker protection in many respects than the patent law. While trade secret law does not forbid the discovery of the trade secret by fair and honest means, *e.g.*, independent creation or reverse engineering, patent law operates "against the world," forbidding any use of the invention for whatever purpose for a significant length of time. The holder of a trade secret also takes a substantial risk that the secret will be passed on to his competitors, by theft or by breach of a confidential relationship, in a manner not easily susceptible of discovery or proof. Where patent law acts as a barrier, trade secret law functions relatively as a sieve. The possibility that an inventor who believes his invention meets the standards of patentability will sit back, rely on trade secret law, and after one year of use forfeit any right to patent protection, is remote indeed.

Nor does society face much risk that scientific or technological progress will be impeded by the rare inventor with a patentable invention who chooses trade secret protection over patent protection. The ripeness-of-time concept of invention, developed from the study of the many independent multiple discoveries in history, predicts that if a particular individual had not made a particular discovery others would have, and in probably a relatively short period of time. If something is to be discovered at all very likely it will be discovered by more than one person. Even were an inventor to keep his discovery completely to himself, something that neither the patent nor trade secret laws forbid, there is a high probability that it will be soon independently developed. If the invention, though still a trade secret, is put into public use, the competition is alerted to the existence of the inventor's solution to the problem and may be encouraged to make an extra effort to independently find the solution thus known to be possible. The inventor faces pressures not only from private industry, but from the skilled scientists who work in our universities and our other great publicly supported centers of learning and research. * * *

* * * Trade secret law and patent law have co-existed in this country for over one hundred years. Each has its particular role to play, and the operation of one does not take away from the need for the other. Trade secret law encourages the development and exploitation of those items of lesser or different invention than might be accorded protection under the patent laws, but which items still have an important part to play in the technological and scientific advancement of the Nation. Trade secret law promotes the sharing of knowledge, and the efficient operation of industry; it permits the individual inventor to reap the rewards of his labor by contracting with a company large enough to develop and expoit it. Congress, by its silence over these many years, has seen the wisdom of allowing the States to enforce trade secret protection. Until Congress takes affirmative action to the contrary, States should be free to grant protection to trade secrets.

Since we hold that Ohio trade secret law is not preempted by the federal patent law, the judgment of the Court of Appeals for the Sixth Circuit is reversed, and the case is remanded to the Court of Appeals with directions to reinstate the judgment of the District Court.

It is so ordered.

■ ■ ■

13

Occupational Safety And Health Act of 1970

Gaylord A. Jentz*

In 1970, after numerous studies and the consistent urging of labor, Congress held hearings on a bill designed to protect one of our most valuable resources, the American worker. Startling statistics were brought out at these hearings. Each year approximately 14,500 workers were being killed, over 2 million workers were being disabled through job-related accidents, and an estimated 300,000 cases of occupational disease were occurring. Human suffering can never be fully measured by any medium, but the national economic loss was overwhelming: over 1.5 billion dollars in lost wages each year, with an 8 billion dollar loss in the gross national product.

State laws relating to worker safety varied substantially, and because state attention to the safety of its workers was at best minimal, Congress passed the Occupational Safety and Health Act of 1970, commonly referred to as OSHA.

PURPOSE

The purpose of the Act is stated as follows: ". . . to assure as far as possible every working man and woman in the Nation safe and healthful working conditions and to preserve our human resources."

To accomplish this purpose, the Act created within the Department of Labor the Occupational Safety and Health Administration (OSHA). This agency is given five specific responsibilities:

(a) to encourage employers and employees to reduce workplace hazards and to implement new or improved existing safety and health programs.

---

*The University of Texas at Austin.

(b) to establish definite responsibilities and rights of employers and employees for the achievement of better safety and health conditions.

(c) to establish procedures for effective monitoring (record keeping and reporting) of job-related illnesses and injuries.

(d) to develop mandatory job safety and health standards and effectively enforce compliance with these standards.

(e) to encourage States to pass legislation and to take over the responsibility of job safety and health within their borders.

COVERAGE

The law applies to any employer engaged in a business affecting commerce. Commerce is broadly defined as any trade, commerce, or communication among the several States, between a State and a foreign country, within the District of Columbia or a possession of the United States, etc. Regardless of occupational field, almost all employers are subject to the Act. It covers professions such as law and medicine, charities and religious organizations, construction, agriculture, and labor organizations, as well as the traditional interstate commerce industrial, wholesale, or retail businesses.

Certain persons or employers are exempt. Family owned and operated farms, self-employed persons, state and local governments as employers, and federal employees whose workplace standards are covered by other Federal statutes are examples of those who are not subject to the Act. However, although Federal agencies are not subject to the Act, these agencies are required to develop job safety and health programs consistent with OSHA standards and to make annual reports to OSHA. If a State wishes to regulate its own safety and health program, state standards and enforcement must be comparable to those of OSHA, and the State program must cover State and local government employees.

ADMINISTRATION

Three federal agencies were created to develop, review, and enforce occupational safety and health standards. They are as follows:

(1) *Occupational Safety and Health Administration - OSHA*

OSHA was created as a component part of the Department of Labor and is the primary administrative agency with authority to promulgate standards, make inspections, and enforce the Act. The Secretary of Labor has three standing advisory committees, which may be called on for recommendations. The three are, the *National Advisory Committee on Occupational Safety and Health* (makes recommendations to the Secretary of Labor and the Secretary of Health, Education, and Welfare on administration of the Act), the *Advisory Committee on Construction Safety and Health* (recommends construction safety and health standards and other industry regulations), and the *Standards Advisory Committee on Agriculture* (recommends standards for the agriculture industry). In addition the Secretary has the power to appoint *ad hoc* committees to recommend standards in other occupational areas. These committees are limited in duration to 270 days.

(2) *National Institute for Occupational Safety and Health - NIOSH*

This agency was created as a component part of the Department of Health, Education, and Welfare. Its primary function is to conduct research on various safety and health problems, provide technical assistance to OSHA, and recommend standards for OSHA to adopt. To fulfull its function, NIOSH has authority to inspect, gather testimony, require employer reports, and have employers provide medical examinations or tests. If medical examinations or tests are required, they are paid for by NIOSH rather than the employer.

(3) *Occupational Safety and Health Review Commission - OSHRC*

This agency is independent of OSHA and is not a part of the Department of Labor. Its primary functions are to assess penalties recommended by OSHA and to handle all appeals from actions taken by OSHA. When an appeal (called a "Notice of Contest") is made, OSHRC assigns an administrative law judge to hear the "contest." OSHRC consists of three persons appointed by the President for staggered six-year terms.

STANDARDS

The Act imposes duties on both employers and employees. The general duty of the employer is to "furnish to each of his employees employment and a place of employment which are free from recognized hazards that are causing or are likely to cause death or serious physical harm to his employees." The duty of the employee is to "comply with all occupational safety and health standards and all rules, regulations, and orders under the Act." To provide the employer and employee a means of meeting their duties, OSHA is responsible for promulgating legally enforceable standards.

There are two kinds of standards:

(1) *Permanent Standards* - When the Act was first passed, the Secretary of Labor was given the authority for a two-year period to establish interim standards. Most standards promulgated during this period were taken from existing standards generally accepted throughout the nation. These standards became permanent.

When OSHA plans to propose new standards or to amend or delete existing standards, a notice of such intention is made in the *Federal Register*. The notice states the proposed change or addition and gives the public at least 30 days from date of publication to respond. This notice is extremely important. Failure to give notice will vacate a proposed standard. If the notice does not provide for a public hearing, interested parties can request one, and OSHA is required to schedule it with an appropriate announcement in the *Federal Register*.

Within 60 days after the close of the comment period or public hearing, whichever is later, OSHA must publish its ruling in the *Federal Register*. If its ruling includes adoption of an amended or new standard, the full text of the standard must be included along with the date the standard becomes effective. The Secretary must include in the publication adequate reasons for a standard's adoption.

If any party affected by a newly adopted standard believes that the standard is vague, inadequate, unnecessary, or burdensome, that party has a right to file an appeal to the appropriate U.S. Circuit Court of Appeals within 60 days of the standard's publication. The filing of appeal does not delay enforcement of the standard unless so directed by the Court.

(2) *Emergency Temporary Standards* - Any time OSHA determines that workers are in serious danger due to any hazard, OSHA is authorized to issue an emergency standard which becomes effective immediately upon publication in the *Federal Register*. Once published, it also becomes a proposed permanent standard and is subject to the procedure for adoption previously discussed. However, a final ruling on a temporary standard must be made within six months or it lapses.

TYPES OF STANDARDS

OSHA standards are available in three volumes—general industry, maritime, and construction. Free single copies are available from OSHA Regional offices upon request. The best method to keep current is to read the *Federal Register* (available by subscription or in some libraries) and to subscribe to the OSHA Subscription Service, a loose-leaf service, available only from the Superintendent of Documents.

Within these three volumes, standards can be considered as general, applying to almost every workplace covered, or specific, applying to a particular machine, production process, or type of business. An example of a general standard is:

Aisles and passageways: (1) Where mechanical handling equipment is used, sufficient safe clearances shall be allowed for aisles, at loading docks, through doorways and wherever turns or passages must be made. Aisles and passageways shall be kept clear and in good repair, with no obstruction across aisles that could create a hazard.

An example of a specific standard is:

Preparing pulpwood: (1) Gang and slasher saws. A guard shall be provided in front of all gang and slasher saws to protect workers from wood thrown by saws. A guard shall be placed over tail sprockets.

Since many standards are written in broad and general terms, a number of cases have emerged claiming that noncompliance citations and penalties assessed violate the due process clause of the Fifth Amendment. As of April,

1978, no OSHA case has been decided by the Supreme Court, but at least six U.S. Courts of Appeal decisions have ruled on the claim of vagueness as a defense.

In some of these cases the statutes are treated as criminal in nature. In criminal cases, statutory language must be specific enough to give persons subject to it "fair warning" of the conduct prohibited. In other litigation, the statutes are treated as civil in nature and require only a test of "customary knowledge," or the test of "whether a reasonable prudent man familiar with the circumstances of the industry would have protected against the hazard."

One of the criticisms of the Act has been what business refers to as "nit-picking" standards. For example, standards covered the size and shape of "exit" signs, "height" of wall mounted fire extinguishers, dimensions of ladders, and even the design of toilet seats. Many of these were initially interim standards approved by private industry groups when the Act was first passed. This year 1,100 "petty" standards were deleted, yet there remain numerous standards which one can seriously question as necessary for protection of employees.

VARIANCE FROM STANDARDS

An employer who is or will be in noncompliance with OSHA standards may make an application for a variance when he feels he has facilities and operations sufficient to provide adequate employee protection. This application is also frequently made when an employer presently lacks the means to comply with standards. There are four types of variances.

(1) *Temporary Variance* - A temporary variance is granted only when an employer who cannot comply with a standard by its effective date can demonstrate through experts that personnel or materials are unavailable, or that construction or alteration of facilities cannot be completed by that date. The employer must establish to OSHA's satisfaction that measures have been taken to protect the employee and that adequate steps have been instituted for coming into compliance. Notice of variance application must be given to the employees stating their right to request a hearing on the application. Temporary variances may be granted for a period up to one year and can be renewed twice for periods of six months. Variances will not be granted because of an employer's financial inability to put his workplace in compliance.

(2) *Permanent Variance* - If an employer can prove that his program and facilities provide as safe a workplace as would compliance with a standard, a permanent variance may be granted. OSHA usually makes an inspection. Employees must be notified of the pending application and their right to request a hearing. If the permanent variance is granted, employees can petition OSHA within six months to modify or revoke the variance. OSHA can take similar steps on its own initiative.

(3) *Experimental Variance* - If an employer is experimenting in new job safety and health techniques approved by either the Secretary of Labor

or Secretary of Health, Education, and Welfare, a variance may be granted to permit the continuance of the experiment. Notice to employees is not required.

(4) *National Defense Variance* - The Secretary of Labor can always grant a variance when in the interest of our national defense.

Variances are not retroactive. Any citations for violations of standards will not be set aside by a later granting of a variance. However, while a variance application is being considered, an employer may apply for and be granted an interim order permitting the employer to operate under existing conditions without citation. This order is published in the *Federal Register*. Notice to employees is required by at least a posting of the order.

INSPECTIONS

Enforcement of standards is accomplished primarily by inspections conducted by OSHA compliance officers. The Act specifically provides that compliance officers are authorized:

(1) to enter without delay at reasonable times any factory, plant, establishment, construction site, or other area, workplace or environment where work is performed by an employee of an employer; and

(2) to inspect and investigate during regular working hours and at other reasonable times, and within reasonable limits and in a reasonable manner, any such place of employment and all pertinent conditions, structures, machines, apparatus, devices, equipment, and materials therein, and to question privately any such employer, owner, operator, agent, or employee.

The compliance officer should display his Department of Labor credentials which bear his name, photograph, and serial number. If identification is not displayed, the employer should insist upon this identification before inspection of the premises. Verification of the identity of a compliance officer can be made by phoning the nearest OSHA Regional Office. The compliance officer is permitted only to inspect the premises, give compliance advice, and recommend citations. The officer is not authorized to assess or collect penalties.

Whether an employer may legally deny a compliance officer's inspection without a proper search warrant has been decided by the Supreme Court. The Fourth Amendment to the U.S. Constitution requires a search warrant, issued upon a showing of probable cause, for inspections of commercial establishments, unless the owner consents to the inspection. The Fourth Amendment's requirement of a search warrant is primarily concerned with the protection of privacy interests.

The Supreme Court, however, permits an exception to the requirement of a search warrant for searches or inspections under three tests. The first is a "pervasive regulation" test that permits warrantless searches of an industry that has a long history of governmental control, such as the liquor and firearm industries. Second is a "statutory restraint" test which allows warrantless searches that are reasonable in time, place, and manner. Third is the "effective enforcement" test that permits warrantless searches where surprise is necessary to effectively enforce the law. The Supreme Court has not as yet decided whether all tests (or combinations thereof) must be met to permit warrantless searches or whether any of the three standing alone will suffice.

Early in 1978, the case of *Marshall* v. *Barlow's Inc.* (424 F. Supp. 437) was appealed to the U.S. Supreme Court. In the *Marshall* case, an Idaho District Court held the inspection provisions of Sec. 8(a) of the Occupational Safety Health Act, which permits warrantless inspections, to be in violation of the Fourth Amendment's ban of unreasonable searches and seizures. On appeal the government argued that when an employer opens a work area to employees, he is precluded from claiming privacy. Further, the government argued that the Act provides only for inspections at reasonable times, reasonable places, and in a reasonable manner.

In a five-to-three decision, the Supreme Court held that an employer can constitutionally bar OSHA from making warrantless inspections. The Court, however, made the warrants easy to obtain. In order to secure a warrant, the inspector must simply show that a specific business is being chosen for inspection on a spot check basis of a general enforcement plan rather than being singled out for arbitrary reasons. Thus the warrant can be obtained in advance without notifying the employer and retain the element of "surprise." The dissenting justices charged that the majority had not only misinterpreted the Fourth Amendment but had weakened the amendment's provision that warrants should be issued only upon a finding of probable cause.

It is estimated that five million workplaces or businesses are coverd by the Act. Approximately 2% of these businesses are inspected on an annual basis. Priority for inspections has been developed.

The first priority for inspection is given to situations where employees are in "imminent" danger of serious physical harm or are subject to health hazards which could cause serious threat to life or irreversible harm by shortened life or physical or mental inefficiency due to exposure. These situations frequently are brought to the attention of OSHA by an employee or by an authorized employee representative. Often the situation becomes apparent from required records reported to OSHA. If an imminent danger is found upon inspection and the employer fails to correct the situation, a suit in Federal District Court may be instituted by OSHA. Should OSHA "arbitrarily or capriciously" refuse to bring such court action, employees concerned can sue the Secretary of Labor to compel him to do so. This could result in a court order shutting down operations of that employer. Under the Act, employees can legally walk off the job where the employer has refused to correct the danger, the employee (under a reasonable person test) believes the danger is so real it will cause death or serious physical harm, and there is no reasonable alternative to a walk-out. The walk-out provisions of the Act conflict with union contracts which carry no-strike clauses and agreements to arbitrate disputes. Arbitration agreements presumably would lock an employee into the arbitration process, rather than permitting him to exercise his right to walk off the job under OSHA.

The second inspection priority is where a catastrophe results in death or hospitalization for five or more employees. Catastrophes must be reported to OSHA within 48 hours of occurrence. These inspections are after the fact to see if standards were violated and to determine what steps need to be taken to avoid similar catastrophes.

The third inspection priority is in response to a valid employee complaint.

Every employee has a right to request in writing an inspection when the employee feels OSHA standards are being violated and dangers or hazards exist. The employee can have his name withheld from the employer. If OSHA determines the complaint to be justified, an inspection will be held. If not, OSHA is required to so notify the employee and, upon request of the employee, to hold an informal review.

The fourth inspection priority is used primarily to monitor high-risk jobs and health occupations, industries, or businesses. These include industries which expose employees to toxic substances or require them to handle extremely volatile or hot materials, and industries where severe injury, illness, or death rates are high.

The fifth inspection priority is the random or routine inspection of all types of business and occupations covered under the Act.

Regardless of the priority, once a business has been inspected and serious violations have been cited, a reinspection is automatically made to determine whether the cited hazard has been corrected.

INSPECTION TOURS

After the compliance officer has displayed proper credentials, an opening conference is held. At this conference the purpose and scope of inspection is explained. Copies of the complaint and relevant standards are given to the employer.

The employer has the right to have a representative accompany the compliance officer on the inspection. The complaining employee or an authorized employee representative also has the right to join the compliance officer on inspection. If there is no employee representative, the compliance officer is required to consult with a reasonable number of employees about safety matters at the workplace.

The inspection process permits the compliance officer to consult with employees in private. An employee can file a discrimination complaint with OSHA, within thirty days of any action by the employer against that employee because of the employee's complaint or participation in an inspection. If OSHA determines the discrimination complaint is valid, the Secretary of Labor has the right to seek legal relief on behalf of the aggrieved employee.

The inspection process usually involves a review of required employer records, a check to see if there is a proper posting of OSHA requirements, and actual observations of the workplace. Some violations can be corrected on the spot, and are so recorded as evidence of an employer's good-faith compliance. Even so, on occasion citations have still been issued and penalties imposed.

At the end of the inspection, the compliance officer holds a closing conference. During the conference the officer discusses the inspection and advises the employer of all violations for which citations may be issued. He does not have the authority to assess penalties.

Generally inspections are conducted without notice. The Act provides for a fine up to $1,000 and/or a 6 month jail term to persons, other than OSHA, alerting an employer to an inspection in advance. OSHA may give advance notice under special circumstances. These include imminent danger situations, inspections which require special preparation or which must be performed after regular hours, and situations where more thorough or effective inspections would be provided if advance notice were given.

It is always possible that upon inspection the compliance officer or others authorized to inspect may obtain trade secret information. The Act treats this information as confidential. Any inspector who releases such information without consent is subject to a $1,000 fine and/or imprisonment up to 1 year.

CITATIONS AND PENALTIES

The compliance officer reports to the OSHA area director what citations, if any, should be issued. The area director decides what citations are to be issued and the period of time the employer has to correct these violations. He also will propose penalties, but only OSHRC can actually assess penalties.

The issued citations and notices of proposed penalties are sent to the employer by certified mail. The employer is required to post a copy of each citation at the place where the violation occurred. This serves as a notice to the employees of the noncompliance situation. The citation must remain posted for at least 3 days or until the violation is corrected, whichever is longer. No citation may be issued "after the expiration of six months following the occurrence of any violation."

The Act defines different types of violations and imposes civil penalties for each class of violation. These can be grouped as follows:

(a) *De Minimis* - Sometimes a standard is violated, but the violation has no direct or immediate relationship to the job safety and health of the employees within an employer's workplace. In such circumstances a notice of violation is issued, but there is no citation or proposed penalty.

(b) *Nonserious Violation* - The Act specifically provides that certain violations may be "determined not to be of a serious nature." A nonserious violation is one which has a direct relationship to job safety and health, but which would probably not result in death or serious harm. Civil penalties of up to $1,000 may be assessed for each violation. These penalties are *discretionary*.

(c) *Serious Violation* - A serious violation exists "if there is a substantial probability that death or serious physical harm could result" from noncompliance and the employer knew or should have known of the hazard. The latter qualification can be very important, particularly where the employer has provided employees with appropriate safety protective equipment with strict instructions requiring the use of such equipment on the job. Violations could occur because employees were not wearing the protective equipment during an inspection. However, violations resulting from individual employee choice, without employer knowledge, should not be treated as serious violations. A number of U.S. Court of Appeals decisions have had to deal, in particular, with penalties imposed upon an employer due to noncompliance by an employee. These decisions seem to indicate four elements are needed for an employer to have a serious violation citation and resulting penalty. They are: (1) failure of an employee to comply with a standard, (2) substantial probability of death or serious harm resulting from such violation, (3) the employer's knowledge or reason to know of the violation, and (4) ability of the employer to take effective and feasible measures to avoid the citation. Civil penalties for serious violations are *mandatory*, up to $1,000 for each violation.

The Act gives OSHRC the authority in assessing penalties to give "due consideration to the appropriateness of the penalty with respect to the size of the business being charged, the gravity of the violation, the good faith of the employer, and the history of previous violations." The Commission has adjusted penalties downward for both types of violation by as much as 50% based on these factors. All penalties owed are to be paid to the Secretary of Labor for deposit in the U.S. Treasury. Enforcement of payment is by an action brought in a Federal District Court where the employer has its principal office.

The Act also specifies other types of violations and penalties. They are as follows:

(a) Any person who knowingly falsifies statements, applications, records, or reports required of the Act shall, upon conviction, be fined not more than $10,000 and/or be imprisoned up to 6 months.

(b) Any person who gives unauthorized advance notice of inspection shall upon conviction be fined up to $1,000 and/or be imprisoned up to 6 months.

(c) Any employer who violates any posting requirements of the Act shall be assessed a civil penalty up to $1,000 for each violation.

(d) Any employer who fails to correct a violation within the abatement period may be assessed a civil penalty of not more than $1,000 for each *day* during which such failure or violation continues.

(e) Criminal actions will be brought against anyone killing, assaulting, resisting, intimidating, or interfering with a compliance officer.

(f) Any employer who "willfully and repeatedly" violates the Act may be assessed a civil penalty of not more than $10,000 for each violation. In addition, if this type of violation results in the death of an employee, upon conviction, the employer shall be fined up to $10,000 and/or imprisoned up to 6 months. A second conviction doubles the maximum penalties.

There has been considerable argument over the effectiveness of these penalties. Seldom has the maximum penalty been imposed. Some labor organizations argue that the penalties are ineffective in bringing workplaces into compliance with job safety and health standards. Penalties assessed for willful violations which result in an employee's death have been said to be absurd, especially when compared to sentences for negligent homicide or manslaughter.

Suits have been filed claiming that the civil penalties provided for by the Act are in reality criminal fines which cannot be assessed without the jury trial guaranteed by the 6th Amendment of the U.S. Constitution. Two U.S. Court of Appeals cases rejected these claims, holding that Congressional intent was clear in constituting OSHA penalties for noncompliance as civil, not criminal penalties. Although no suit has been filed claiming a right to trial by jury for OSHA violations under the 7th Amendment of the U.S. Constitution, previous U.S. Supreme Court decisions have clearly made trial by jury inapplicable to administrative adjudications where Congress has designated the tribunal of enforcement.

APPEAL

Both employers and employees have a right to appeal or contest certain actions and decisions made under the Act. The employee's rights of appeal are greatly limited—in part, because the major thrust of the Act is to hold the employer responsible for the job safety and health of his employees. Employees therefore cannot contest or appeal citations. But employees can object to the abatement time alloted to the employer by the OSHA area director for correction of a violation if they file with OSHA a written objection within 15 *working* days of the employer's receipt of a citation. This objection acts as an appeal and is forwarded to OSHRC for review.

Employees who have filed an OSHA complaint can request an *informal* review conference of any OSHA decision not to issue a citation. Such reviews may also be requested of OSHA to discuss citations, proposed penalties, and employer appeals. These are obviously informational exchanges and not part of an appeal process.

The employer can appeal the citation, the period of abatement, or the proposed penalty by written notification to the OSHA area director within 15 working days of the receipt of the citation. This is called a "Notice of Contest." A copy of the "Notice of Contest" must be given to the authorized employees' representative. If there is no representative, the notice must be posted in a prominent place or be personally delivered to the employees. The "Notice" must clearly identify the basis of the appeal, state how such notice was given to the employees, and inform employees of their right to participate in the OSHRC proceedings.

The OSHA area director forwards the appeal to OSHRC, which in turn assigns the contest to an administrative law judge for disposition. Unless the appeal is legally invalid, a hearing is held. Employer and employees have a right to participate. The judge makes findings of fact and conclusions of law affirming, modifying, or vacating the actions of the OSHA area director. Within 30 days of the judge's decision, any party or an OSHRC commissioner may seek further review by OSHRC. Any final administrative ruling can be appealed to the appropriate U.S. Court of Appeals.

A failure to file a "Notice of Contest" is not subject to review by any court or agency. It has been held that where the employer files a "Notice of Contest" challenging the penalty, but not the citation, the cited violation is not subject to review.

RECORDS AND REPORTS

Employers with eleven or more employees must maintain records of occupational injuries and illnesses as they occur. Except for job related accidents which result in death or hospitalization of five or more employees (where the law requires a reporting to the nearest OSHA office within 48 hours), records of occupational injury or illness must be kept at the location where the business is conducted or where the employee services are performed.

All occupational injuries and illnesses must be recorded if they result in death, one or more lost work days, medical treatment (other than first aid), restriction of motion, unconsciousness, or transfer to another job. For most businesses, three recordkeeping forms were initially required. Recently OSHA has combined two of these rather long, complicated forms into one brief form (reducing 80 entries to 19). This action affects approximately 1.5 million large businesses and is in response to industry criticism and adverse legal decisions.

WORKMEN'S COMPENSATION

The Act created a National Commission on State Workman's Compensation laws. The purpose of this Commission was to make a comprehensive study of State Workmen's Compensation laws to determine if such laws are adequate in awarding compensation for job related injuries and illnesses. The Commission has filed a final report and has been discharged. It is important to note that OSHA does not affect an employee's right to workmen's compensation benefits.

STATE APPROVED PLANS BY OSHA

The Act permits and encourages States to develop and enforce their own job safety and health programs. When, for a period of three years, these programs are "at least as effective in providing safe and healthful employment and places of employment" as existing under Federal regulation, OSHA can approve a State plan submitted. Once approved, the State rather than OSHA will become the primary enforcement body subject to OSHA evaluation and reports. If the State programs fall below the level of effectiveness required, OSHA can begin its own enforcement or take action to withdraw approval of the State program.

FEDERAL AID TO SMALL BUSINESS

The Act amended the Small Business Act by permitting eligible small businesses to apply for long term assistance loans (through the Small Business Administration) to place their workplaces in compliance with OSHA standards. These loans are to be awarded only if the SBA determines that the small business "is likely to suffer substantial economic injury without assistance."

ISSUES CONFRONTING OSHA

There are many issues still confronting OSHA which must be resolved before critics can be silenced and proponents satisfied with the Act. Some issues will probably never be fully resolved.

The biggest single issue is the effectiveness of the Act. Occupational injuries and illnesses have not substantially decreased, and in some areas are on the rise. Labor Department statistics show that the incidence of injuries rose from 8.8 per hundred workers in 1975 to 8.9 in 1976. Serious injury and illness rose from 3.3 to 3.5 per hundred workers and working days lost rose from 56.2 days to 60.5 days per hundred workers during the same period. Deaths rose in service industries but declined in the wholesale and retail trades. Generally, overall incidence of injuries and illnesses rose in such industries as manufacturing, agriculture, public utilities, transportation, forestry and fishing, but declined in others such as the wholesale, and the finance, insurance, and real estate trades. Although numerous reasons are given, in eight years the Act, as presently written and enforced, has not accomplished its stated purpose.

Another controversy involves the number of inspections made (too often after the fact) and the qualifications of inspectors. Although increased budgets and better training have permitted more meaningful inspections, labor remains critical of the lack of inspection and the employer of the "unqualified" or "nit-picking" inspector.

The number and generality of standards have caused confusion, law suits, distrust, and strong critical comment of the Act. Although some standards (called "nit-picking") have been deleted, many more deserve the same fate or need amendment. Standards which do little to protect the worker have become the subject of jokes and sources of irritation to employers.

The Act does little to affect the behavior of employees. It is the employee, rather than the workplace, which frequently is the cause of his own injury or the injury of another. The employer is expected to police the employee or be subject to penalty. There is no incentive for the employee to comply with the Act and no penalty for noncompliance.

Many have criticized the research efforts under the Act, particularly the slowness in developing standards to control occupational illnesses or diseases such as cancer, or infertility. This criticism is highlighted when employee complaints and/or records would indicate swifter action.

In addition to these issues, others have been mentioned earlier in the chapter. The issue concerning the necessity of the search warrant will perhaps soon be resolved. The effectiveness of the present penalties will have to be evaluated. The issues of jury trials and civil versus criminal penalties seem to have been resolved.

The purpose of the Act is still most creditable, and the need for job injury and illness records is obvious. It is a shame that in eight years, the procedures and enforcement have created more controversy than results.

14

Employment Discrimination

Fred J. Naffziger*

With the passage of the 1964 Civil Rights Act, the federal government began a major effort to eliminate discriminatory employment practices. That effort continues today. In this chapter we will examine several of the more important civil rights statutes and some of the important legal and social issues that they pose.

THE CIVIL RIGHTS ACT OF 1964

The most important legislation prohibiting employment discrimination is Title VII of the 1964 Civil Rights Act as amended by the 1972 Equal Employment Opportunity Act. The amended Act makes it unlawful to discriminate against an individual because of his or her race, color, religion, sex or national origin. The law applies to an employer in any industry affecting commerce that has 15 or more employees. It applies to any labor organization (union) that has 15 or more members or which operates a hiring hall. Employment agencies are also governed by the law. The statutes apply to state and local governments, and to their political subdivisions, but not to employees of the federal government. These latter individuals have the right to equal employment opportunity under other laws. Finally, Executive Order 11246 forbids discrimination by contractors and subcontractors that do business with the federal government.

Under the present law, it is an unlawful employment practice for an employer to fail or refuse to hire or to discharge any individual or otherwise to discriminate against any individual with respect to his or her compensation, or other terms, conditions, or privileges of employment because of such in-

*University of Texas at Arlington

dividual's race, color, religion, sex, or national origin. It is likewise unlawful for a labor organization to exclude or to expel from its membership or otherwise to discriminate against any individual on the basis of those five factors.

RELIGIOUS AND NATIONAL ORIGIN DISCRIMINATION

The First Amendment to the U.S. Constitution guarantees individuals the free exercise of religion and prohibits the government from establishing a religion. To prevent the Civil Rights Act of 1964 from running afoul of the Constitution a provision was inserted stating that it is not unlawful for a religious organization to hire employees of a particular religion to perform work connected with carrying on its activities. Thus, the Catholic Church can legally refuse to hire anyone other than members of the Catholic faith as teachers in its parochial schools.

Individuals who, because of their religious beliefs, find it impossible to work after sundown Friday, or on Saturday, have little protection. Employers have a statutory obligation to make a reasonable accommodation for the religious observance or practice of its employees, short of incurring an undue hardship. Consider an individual whose religion regards Saturday as the Sabbath and forbids work on the Sabbath. He has insufficient seniority to bid for a shift with Saturdays off. He refuses to work on Saturday and is subsequently discharged. The union will not allow any violation of the seniority system. The company refuses to permit him to work a four day week or to replace him with a supervisor or other worker on the fifth day. It also refuses to fill his Saturday slot by calling in an individual for overtime. Finally, it refuses to work out a swap with another employee on a different shift because this would violate the seniority provisions of the collective bargaining agreement. Does the discharge of this employee violate the law? No. The Supreme Court has held that the employer had made a reasonable effort to accommodate the employee's religious practices and each alternative, which had been rejected, would have imposed an undue hardship on the employer.[1]

With regard to the bar against using the national origin of an individual as the basis for discrimination, an employer could not refuse to hire Cuban-Americans because he disliked the Cuban government or disliked people with Spanish accents. However, it is not illegal to discriminate against aliens; a company is free to adopt a policy of hiring only U.S. citizens.[2]

SEX DISCRIMINATION

Most sex discrimination cases involve allegations that a company or union is discriminating against a woman because of her sex. This discussion will focus on situations of this nature. One important caveat: it is illegal to discriminate against a man because of his sex.

What the law does not allow is disparate treatment of males and females based upon sex. For example, suppose a company rejects women job applicants, who have preschool children, when it has no policy which bars the employment of men with preschool children. This is violative of the statute. So too is requiring the female employees to be married while not requiring marriage of the male workers. What is illegal in both instances is the unequal treatment based upon sex. If a company wishes to exclude from its workforce all individuals with preschool children, it may legally do so. It is also unlawful for a company and union to establish sexually segregated seniority lists that exclude women from bidding on certain jobs, e.g., a job that requires the worker to lift 35 pounds or more. The assumption that all men are capable of performing such tasks and therefore are eligible to bid on the job, while all or most women are incapable of such lifting and are thereby ineligible, is legally faulty. All individuals, regardless of their sex, must be given the opportunity to demonstrate their ability to perform such a job.[3] If a woman demonstrates the requisite capability, she is not to be denied the job simply because she is a woman.

Women's groups are very disturbed by several Supreme Court decisions involving pregnancy related issues. In 1976 the Court ruled that an employer does not violate Title VII's ban on sex discrimination when it denies benefits for pregnancy related disabilities under its disability income protection plan.[4] The position of the Court is that such a plan does not exclude anyone from benefit eligibility because of gender but merely removes one physical condition--pregnancy--from the list of compensable disabilities. The court says that such an exclusion is not a pretext for discriminating against women, since pregnancy, though confined to women, is in other ways significantly different from the typical covered disease or disability. Congress is considering legislation which would overturn this decision. In the meantime, the Court has used the case for a decision in 1977 holding that an employer's policy of not awarding sick leave pay to pregnant employees is not *per se* a violation of Title VII. However, it did say the denial of accumulated seniority to employees returning from pregnancy leave is a violation.[5] On constitutional due process grounds the Court held in 1974 that a woman cannot be forced by her employer to take a maternity leave at an arbitrary cut-off date; she may work as long as her doctor believes work to be medically safe.[6]

Some employers have minimum height and weight standards that job applicants must meet. What is the legal status of such qualification requirements that seem to be neutral? If they in fact work so as to disproportionately exclude women from employment they violate the '64 Act. Alabama had a minimum height requirement of 5'2" and a minimum weight of 120 pounds for its prison guards. If one considers all the individuals in the U.S. between the ages of 18-79, these restrictions taken together exclude 41.13% of the female population from employment but exclude less than one percent of the male population. These requirements were struck down as unlawful discrimination.[7]

Let us quickly examine the issue of sexual harrassment on the job. If a male supervisor conditions favorable job evaluations and promotions for a female employee upon her grant of sexual favors, does that constitute illegal sex discrimination? While there is some legal confusion as to the answer, the trend appears to be that such a practice is a violation of Title VII if the subordinate employee's job status depends upon a favorable response to the sexual demands and the employer does not take prompt and appropriate remedial action after becoming aware of the situation.[8] Keep in mind that this would also apply with a female supervisor and a male subordinate.

142

Finally, the law does not prohibit discrimination against an individual on grounds of homosexuality.

BONA FIDE OCCUPATIONAL QUALIFICATIONS

It is not an unlawful employment practice for an employer, union or employment agency to judge an individual upon his or her religion, sex, or national origin in those specific instances where religion, sex or national origin is a bona fide occupational qualification (bfoq), reasonably necessary to the normal operation of that particular enterprise. Discrimination based upon one's race or color is always illegal.

The bfoq is an extremely narrow exception to the law. The guidelines of the Equal Employment Opportunity Commission cite the occupation of actor or actress as being one. They provide that one cannot utilize stereotyped sexual characterizations in the hiring decision--for example the idea that men are less capable then women of assembling intricate equipment; that women lack the aggressiveness necessary for successful sales personnel; or that women have a greater job turnover rate than do men. Being female is not a bfoq for a job as an airline cabin attendant; a male can perform the tasks just as well. The fact that customers overwhelmingly prefer females as cabin attendants is irrelevant.[9] The Supreme Court has ruled that being male is a bfoq for a prison guard in a maximum security prison where the prison system is characterized by such rampant violence that a court has held the conditions to be constitutionally intolerable; twenty per cent of the male prisoners are sex offenders scattered throughout the general prison population; inmates have access to the guards because of dormitory living arrangements; and the institution is understaffed. The Court said this factual situation leads to a security problem directly linked to the sex of the prison guard.[10]

It is not unlawful for an employer to apply different standards of compensation, or different terms, conditions, or privileges of employment pursuant to a bona fide seniority or merit system, or pursuant to a system which measures earnings by quantity or quality of production, nor is it unlawful for an employer to apply different standards to employees who work in different locations, provided that such differences are not the result of an intention to unlawfully discriminate.

RACE OR COLOR DISCRIMINATION

The civil rights statutes do not guarantee individuals a job regardless of their qualifications. Instead, they prohibit the erection of artificial or discriminatory obstacles in the path of job applicants or employees. It is illegal to hire a lesser qualified white over a more qualified black; or to hire a lighter skinned black over a darker skinned but better qualified black. Many of the early discrimination cases involved just such blatant discrimination. With the passage of time, discrimination became more subtle and sophisticated. Questions arose over ostensibly neutral employment practices that have a disproportionate impact upon certain minority groups, and the issue of what remedial action is available to overcome the effects of past discriminatory behavior presented itself in various forms.

The '64 Act contains a clause stating that it is not unlawful for an employer to give and to act upon the results of any professionally developed ability test, so long as the test is neither designed nor used to discriminate on grounds of race, color, religion, sex, or national origin. The Supreme Court has interpreted this clause to mean that such tests must be "job related". Consider a requirement that an individual must pass an aptitude test to be hired or to secure a job transfer. Suppose these tests, although neutral on their face, render ineligible a markedly disproportionate number of blacks, while not measuring an applicant's ability to perform a particular job. In holding such tests to be unlawfully discriminatory, the Court noted that they were not job related for they did not bear a demonstrable relationship to successful performance of the job.[11]

Title VII contains a rigorous statutory standard that requires a probing judicial review of job requirements. The Supreme Court has held that a less rigorous standard applies under the Due Process Clause of the Fifth Amendment. Two unsuccessful black applicants to the District of Columbia police force claimed that the department's recruiting procedures, including a written personnel test, were racially discriminatory in violation to the due process clause. The court concluded that absent a racially discriminatory purpose, a sufficiently validated test is not unconstitutional solely because it has a racially disproportionate impact (four times as many blacks as whites failed the test).[12]

Seniority is of crucial importance in the workplace. The last hired, first fired formula is traditional and determines who is to be laid off in times of economic retrenchment. It also determines, such questions as the order of job recalls, who can advance by bidding for other job openings within the plant, and who gets first choice of work shifts. Problems arise when an individual, e.g., a woman or minority group member, has low seniority attributable to previous illegal discrimination. To cure the effects of the prior discrimination, retroactive seniority and backpay can be granted to these employees.[13] A person can be awarded retroactive seniority without formally applying for a position if he can meet the difficult burden of proving that he would have applied for the job had it not been for the employer's unlawful discriminatory employment practices. However, an otherwise neutral bona fide seniority system does not become unlawful under Title VII simply because it may perpetuate the effects of discrimination that occurred prior to the enactment of the '64 Act.[14]

REVERSE DISCRIMINATION

Probably the most controversial civil rights issue in the late nineteen seventies is the question of reverse discrimination. As women and minority group members make advances in employment, some white males believe that they are the victims of reverse discrimination--that sex and color, not merit or ability, determine some employment decisions to their detriment.

One section of the Civil Rights Act states that an employer, union, or employment agency is not required to grant preferential treatment to any individual or to any group in order to correct an imbalance of persons of any race, color, religion, sex, or national origin by bringing the number of employees or union members into line with the percentage of such individuals in some supposed relevant geographical area. Further, the Fourteenth Amendment guarantees persons equal protection of the laws.

Many of the early reverse discrimination cases revolved around the affirmative action plans required to be adopted by contractors and subcontractors for them to gain eligibility for work on federally financed construction projects. Typically, these would establish specific goals for the hiring of minority workers--goals based upon the minority group's percentage of representation in the construction industry in a given geographical area. While acknowledging that such plans were "color-conscious," courts would uphold them on the basis that the civil rights law was not passed to freeze the status quo and does not outlaw remedial action to overcome existing evils.[15]

Most of the current controversy is generated by the *Bakke* case.[16] The University of California at Davis has 100 seats available each year for its entering medical school class. Eighty-four of those admitted go through a normal admission program. The remaining sixteen seats in the class are filled by means of a special minority admissions process. Only members of minority races are eligible for consideration under the special admissions program. The two groups of applicants are rated separately and are not rated against each other. In both 1973 and 1974 Mr. Bakke, a white male, applied but was denied admission under the normal admission process. Some of the students admitted through the special admissions program had ratings below that of Bakke, who was rejected. The California Supreme Court said that the issue is whether a racial classification intended to help minorities, which also deprives non-minorities of benefits they would enjoy but for their race, violates the constitutional rights of the majority. In the California Court's view in order to be legal such classification must serve a compelling state interest and there must be no other reasonable way to achieve the designated goals by means of lesser restrictions on the non-favored group. Between 1969-74 only eight per cent of the medical students in the U.S. were Black, Indian, Chicano, or Puerto Rican. The university justified its minority admissions program as necessary to integrate the medical school and profession and to serve the minority community. The court held that these arguments do not meet the legal test of a compelling state interest. It also noted that the university need not rely solely upon test scores for admission, but could utilize interviews, character references, the applicants' potential, etc., in selecting its student body. It said that because there was no evidence that the university had discriminated in the past, there was no need for remedial measures. It held that the admission process violates the Constitutional rights of non-minority applicants because it affords preference on the basis of race to persons who by the university's own standards are not as qualified as non-minorities denied admission. A U.S. Supreme Court decision in the matter is pending as of Spring 1978.

One Supreme Court decision does hold that Title VII of the Civil Rights Act prohibits racial discrimination against white persons just as it prohibits racial discrimination against nonwhites.[17] In this case, two white employees and one black employee misappropriated cargo from one of the employer's shipments. The two white employees were discharged. The court noted that while theft may be the basis for discharging an employee, members of all races must have the same criterion for discharge applied to them. Under Title VII, both the company and the union involved were held subject to liability for the discharge.

THE EQUAL EMPLOYMENT OPPORTUNITY COMMISSION

A major mechanism for enforcing compliance with the 1964 and 1972 civil rights laws is the Equal Employment Opportunity Commission (EEOC). Before an individual who believes himself to be the victim of illegal discrimination can resort to a lawsuit, he must first utilize the administrative processes of EEOC. The individual must file the charge within 180 days of the alleged discrimination, unless it was first filed with a state or local agency. In the latter instance, the charge must be filed with EEOC within 300 days of the alleged violation or 30 days after the state or local agency has terminated its proceedings, whichever is earlier. EEOC notifies the organization of the discrimination charges filed against it. If, after an investigation, EEOC believes a violation has occurred, it seeks to settle the case through a confidential process of voluntary conciliation. If this proves impossible, EEOC can bring suit (including a class action lawsuit) in an effort to force the cessation of the alleged unlawful employment practice. Most states have their own fair employment practice law and a state enforcement agency. In these states the discrimination charge must first be filed with the state agency. The individual is free to file charges with EEOC only after the charges have been on file with the state for a minimum of 60 days. The individual is free to bring a private lawsuit if EEOC dismisses the charge or if 180 days have elapsed without EEOC's having achieved a conciliation agreement or filed suit. If an individual's lawsuit is successful, the defendant can be ordered to pay the plaintiff's legal fees. The major criticism of EEOC is its inability to expeditiously handle its large volume of cases. Its current backlog of unresolved charges exceeds 100,000.

It is unlawful for an employer, union, or employment agency to discriminate against a person because he opposed any unlawful employment practice or made a charge, testified, assisted, or participated in any manner in an investigation, proceeding or hearing under the civil rights law.

THE EQUAL PAY ACT

For many years our society reflected the idea that a man performing the same job as a woman should receive a higher salary because of his role in society. The 1963 Equal Pay Act declares this policy illegal and mandates equal pay for equal work.

The Act prohibits an employer from discriminating "between employees on the basis of sex by paying wages to employees at a rate less than the rate at which he pays wages to employees of the opposite sex for equal work on jobs the performance of which requires equal skill, effort, and responsibility, and which are performed under similar working conditions". The phrase "equal work" as interpreted by the courts does not mean that the jobs must be identical for discriminations to occur. The jobs need be only substantially equal. For example, consider a company that pays its men 21¢ per hour more than women doing the same work because, during periodic line shutdowns, it can assign the men to the performance of tasks included in another job classification that pays 2¢ per hour more than the women's wage rate. Even when the men are infrequently assigned this work, they retain their higher hourly pay rate. A court has held these jobs to be substantially equal.[18] Whenever an unlawful wage differential does exist, the statute requires the employer to raise the pay of those being discriminated against to the higher wage level of those performing equal work. In this case the employer had to pay the women $901,062 in back pay. The statute disallows the utilization of artificial job classifications to avoid the law. The courts are not bound by job descriptions; they examine the actual job content.

Exceptions exist that will permit different payment to employees of the opposite sex pursuant to a) a seniority system; b) a merit system; c) a system which measures earnings by quantity or quality of production; or d) a differential based on any other factor other than sex. Once it is shown that an employer pays workers of one sex more than workers of the opposite sex for equal work, the burden shifts to the employer to show that the differential is justified under one of these exceptions. If a company pays personnel in a bona fide training program a higher salary for performing the same work as those not in the program the differential is allowable. Or, the higher profitability of a store's men's department will justify paying its salespeople a higher salary than that earned by the sales staff in a lower profit women's department.[19] The wage differential is based on a factor other than sex; it is based on the economic factor of profitability.

The Act governs every employee who is covered by the federal minimum wage law, plus many executive, administrative, sales and professional employees who are exempt from the minimum wage provisions.

AGE DISCRIMINATION

The Age Discrimination in Employment Act of 1967 bars employers, labor organizations and employment agencies from discriminating against individuals between the ages of 40 and 65 because of their age. In the Spring of 1978 a bill was awaiting final Congressional action which would, with several minor exceptions, raise the maximum age limit from 65 to 70.

The Act applies to employers of 20 or more employees in an industry affecting commerce. Unions that have 25 members or more or operate a hiring hall are covered, as are employment agencies regardless of their size. The employees of state and local governments, as well as those of many federal agencies, are protected by the Act. An employer cannot refuse to hire or to discharge a person or discriminate against him with respect to compensation, terms, conditions, or privileges of employment because of that individual's age. A union cannot exclude, expel, or otherwise discriminate against such a person on account of his age. An employment agency cannot discriminate against, or refuse to refer an individual for employment because of the person's age.

One's age can be the basis for discrimination where age is a bona fide occupational qualification (bfoq) reasonably necessary to the normal operation of the particular business. Age can be a bfoq when factors of safety are involved. Greyhound refused to hire intercity bus drivers over 35 years of age. The court said that if Greyhound could prove that elimination of its maximum hiring age would minimally increase a likelihood of risk of harm to its passengers, then age would be a bfoq.[20] It successfully proved its case by showing: 1) the physical rigors and mental demands of the type of driving assigned to new drivers for many years; 2) that degenerative physical and sensory changes caused by the aging process begin in the late thirties and; 3) that its safest drivers have 16 to 20 years of experience and are between 50 and 55 years of age, a mix unattainable if applicants 40 years of age and over are hired. The Secretary of Labor had unsuccessfully argued that applicants should be judged on their "functional age", the ability to perform the job, rather than their chronological age. The court rejected this saying that it is not clear that functional age is readily determinable. Another court has held that age is not a bfoq for a test pilot where the employer's evidence related to changes that accompany the aging process in the general population while the employee's evidence tended to show that the aging process occurs more slowly and to a lesser degree among pilots and that the accident rate decreases with age.[21]

It is not illegal to act where the different treatment of individuals is based on reasonable factors other than age, or to observe the terms of a bona fide seniority system or any bona fide employee benefit plan, such as a retirement, pension, or insurance plan, which is not a subterfuge to evade the purposes of the Act.

In regard to the benefit plan exception, the Supreme Court has held that it is not unlawful to involuntarily retire a 60 year old employee under the terms of a bona fide retirement plan established in 1941.[22]

The Secretary of Labor enforces both the Equal Pay and Age Discrimination Act. (In early 1978, President Carter proposed shifting this responsibility to EEOC). The voluntary settlement of disputes is encouraged and a voluntary settlement must be sought before a lawsuit is filed. If the Secretary declines to bring suit, the individual can bring a private lawsuit. If the suit is successful, the court can order the defendant to pay, in addition to damages, the reasonable attorney's fees of the plaintiff.

ENDNOTES

1. T.W.A. v. Hardison, 45 LW 4672 (1977).
2. Espinoza v. Farah, 414 U.S. 86(1973).
3. Bowe v. Colgate Palmolive, 416 F2d 711(1970).
4. G.E. v. Gilbert, 429 U.S. 125(1976).
5. Nashville Gas Co. v. Satty, 46 LW 4026(1977).
6. Cleveland Bd. of Ed. v. LaFleur, 414 U.S. —(1974).
7. Dothard v. Rawlinson, 45 LW 4888(1977).

148

8. Tomkins v. Public Service Gas & Elec., 46 LW 2332(1977 CA 3).
9. Diaz v. Pan Am, 442 F2d 385(1971).
10. Supra, note 7.
11. Griggs v. Duke Power Co., 401 U.S. 424(1971).
12. Washington v. Davis, 426 U.S. 229(1976).
13. Albermarle v. Moody, 422 U.S. 405 (1975) (backpay); Franks v. Bowman 424 U.S. 747 (1976) (seniority).
14. Teamsters v. U.S., 45 LW 4506(1977).
15. See Contractors v. Sec. Labor, 442 F2d 159(1971).
16. Bakke v. Regents of U. of Calif., 553 P2d 1152(1976).
17. McDonald v. Santa Fe Trails, 44 LW 5067(1976).
18. Shultz v. Wheaton Glass, 421 F2d 589(1973).
19. Hodgson v. Robert hall, 473 F2d 589 (1973).
20. Hodgson v. Greyhound, 499 F2d 859(1974).
21. Houghton v. McDonnel Douglas, 553 F2d 561(1977).
22. United Air Lines v. McMann, 46 LW 4043(1977).

15

Franchising and the Law

Charles M. Hewitt*

WHY FRANCHISING HAS BECOME A GROWTH INDUSTRY

Franchising is an increasingly important component of the American economy. In 1978 it is estimated that the sales through franchise outlets will approach $300 billion dollars, up 13% from 1977. There are now about 468,000 franchise outlets dispensing both goods and services in the national markets.[1]

A franchise system has been defined in marketing-managment terms as ". . . an organization composed of distributive units established and administered by a supplier as a medium for expanding and controlling the marketing of his products. It is an integrated business system. Franchises are legally independent but economically dependent units of the system.[2]

The franchise approach offers a supplier a highly effective means of gaining rapid market expansion with minimum capital outlay. The growth rate and profitability of many franchise systems has been fantastic. Since most franchisees have the major investment in their outlets, strong profit, and loss incentives are present. Some of the possible advantages of franchising to the franchisor include:

1. By giving exclusive territories and by protecting their franchisees from competition therein, the franchisors are able to attract higher-grade and financially stronger firms into their distribution network.

2. Where goods are involved, production usually must be planned months in advance of delivery. It is much easier to get accurate estimates of future requirements from a selected dealer operation in a "protected market." This gives the franchisors better production control and helps to protect the retail price structure.

*Indiana University

3. By dealing with a few selected retail outlets, the manufacturers can reduce both their selling costs (fewer customer calls) and their transportation costs (larger shipments).

4. By selling to a limited number of retail outlets, each franchisor can give franchisees sufficient volume in their respective market areas of responsibility so that it is possible for the franchisor to insist that each franchisee handle only the franchisor's products and services. This will probably result in a more vigorous and concentrated selling effort being made by the franchisees. It also gives each franchisor a "closed market" for parts and accessories, services and other supplies.

5. By having only a limited number of franchisee-outlets, the franchisor is in a better position to regulate and control retail activities. This is particularly true in view of the fact that the franchisee usually must make a sizeable specialized investment in order to obtain the franchise. The franchisor then has the threat of termination or non-renewal of the franchise as a means of securing franchisee adherence to his basic marketing policies. If terminated, the franchisee may not only lose his business but also the bulk of his investment.

6. By having fewer and financially stronger retail outlets, it is possible for franchisors to require more extensive investments in buildings, stock inventories, and equipment by franchisees; and (to some degree) the franchisors have more assurance that adequate consumer service will be renderd after sale if they use a selected (and typically exclusive) sales agency marketing method. Adequate service after sale has always been essential to retaining customer good will in many franchising industries.

7. By standardizing operating procedures, products, services, and the appearances of outlets, extensive public recognition and acceptance is possible, and so is cost savings.

While the degree and quality of control over the distributive system exercised by the franchisor usually is a decisive factor in determining the degree of success that the system achieves,[3] the purpose and method of control raises some very complex and perplexing issues in many areas of law.

Since the franchisor has in effect put all or most of his distributive eggs in a limited number of baskets, it is understandable that franchisors expect and demand results from franchisees. It is also understandable that franchisee resistance to this franchisor pressure can lead to conflict in marketing channels. From the franchisee's viewpoint the franchise system makes many special aids available. In franchise relationships, however, the distinction between franchisor "assistance" and franchisor "coercion" is sometimes difficult to distinguish.

CHARACTERISTICS OF TYPICAL FRANCHISES

Although franchise differences are great between industries, the franchises used by different franchisors in the same industry usually are markedly similar. The industrial revolution led to an age of mass production and mass markets. The key to success in this industrial age is the word "standardization." It is only logical that firms producing standardized goods, with standardized tools and standardized processes, should seek to standardize their distribution methods.

DURATION

For new franchisees and even for experienced franchisees in some industries, one-year franchise agreements are fairly common. Oil jobbers and service station lessee-operators usually have one-year leases and supply contracts, and one-year franchises are common in the appliance industry. Many such one-year agreements contain "ever-green" clauses that automatically renew the agreement unless advanced notice of non-renewal is given by either party.

Other franchises are of indefinite duration but typically contain express provisions giving either party the right to cancel the arrangement. The notice period may vary from immediate cancellation (coin-machine franchise) to 10 days (soft-drink franchise) to 30 days (a refrigerator-and-appliance franchise) to 90 days (automobile-dealer franchise).

TERRITORY

Most franchises designate a territory in which dealers will be primarily responsible for sales. In earlier franchise agreements dealers often were given exclusive selling rights in designated "protected" territories. Sales "location" clauses prohibiting franchisees from selling the franchised goods or services except from the designated franchised outlets were in common use. Many franchises prohibited the franchisees from selling to "unauthorized" re-sellers such as discount houses.

Serious antitrust questions concerning the validity of vertical marketing restraints were created by the *Schwinn* case.[4] In that case the Supreme Court held that nearly all types of vertical marketing restraints imposed on independent dealers and distributors by franchisors were illegal *per se*. More recently, in the *Sylvania* case, the Supreme Court overruled the *Schwinn per se* rule as applied to vertical restraints except perhaps where the vertical restraints might substantially affect price competition.[5] Non-price vertical restraints such as location clauses (limiting franchisee sales to designated outlets) and exclusive sales territory clauses are now to be tested by "rule of reason" criteria based on their competitive purpose and effect. It is anticipated that many franchisors may now experiment with various types of vertical marketing controls under this less stringent ruling, because strict liability trends in tort law and various recent "consumer protection" laws have imposed increasing legal accountability on franchisors for the quality of the goods and services being delivered to ultimate customers and consumers. Vertical distribution control is important for both marketing strategy and legal liability reasons.

EXCLUSIVE DEALING AND TYING AGREEMENTS

Until recent years many franchises required that dealers handle only products produced, "authorized," or "approved" by their manufacturers. Antitrust problems arise concerning the validity of exclusive dealing contracts where employed by dominant franchisors or where sizeable franchisee markets are being foreclosed to competitors. In general, exclusive dealing agreements are not illegal when employed by franchisors accounting for no more than 2 to 5 percent of a given competitive market.[6]

Much of the antitrust litigation in the franchise area has involved tying contracts where a franchisor conditions the sale of product A (or service A) on the franchisee's purchase of product B (or service B). Where a franchisor has a unique or preferred product or service, the franchisor often is tempted to expand the sales of weaker products or services by tying them in package deals to the stronger product or service. Nearly all tying arrangements are illegal unless there are clear technological or consumer protection considerations present which justify their anticompetitive effect. [7] For example, an ice cream franchisor required that all franchisees buy all of their ice cream mix from the franchisor as a condition for obtaining the franchise and the use of the trademark. The court ruled that this particular tie-in was justified to protect consumer expectations in regard to the product.[8]

INDEFINITENESS OF TERMS

Many franchises do not stipulate a definite amount of goods that the franchisor agrees to deliver and that the franchisee agrees to buy. This failure to stipulate amounts is in part due to economic uncertainties inherent in a dynamic marketing arrangement. In many cases neither the franchisor nor the franchisee can estimate with any reasonable degree of accuracy the volume of products that can or will be sold to consumers.

The court cases and other franchise provisions suggest there may be additional legal reasons for this failure to spell out the obligations of each party to the franchise. Many franchisees have lost lawsuits against their franchisors on the ground that the franchises were so indefinite in their terms that they were unenforceable as contracts. Some franchises appear to be deliberately drawn so as to provide the franchisor with the defense of indefiniteness in the event of suit by the franchisee.[9]

NATURE OF RELATIONSHIP

The legal classification of the relationship between franchisor and franchisee can be extremely important. The courts usually have ruled that the choice in each case rests between a finding that the franchisee is either an agent or an "independent" buyer. The key tests turn on the degree and type of control exercised by the franchisor and on the risk distribution effected by the particular franchise arrangement. In general, the greater the degree of control and risk retained by the franchisor the more likely the relationship will be classed as an agency.

The following situations illustrate how important this question of legal classification becomes in particular instances:

> If a particular franchisee is legally classified as an agent of the franchisor this could make the franchisor legally responsible for all of the franchisee's acts in operating the franchise.[10]

> If the franchisee is an agent the franchisor's tax liability might increase substantially.[11]

> If the franchisee is an agent the franchisor might be in a position to control the franchisee's selling prices or practices with minimum risks under the antitrust laws.[12]

> If the franchisee is an agent the franchisor might have additional legal duties to compensate the franchisee in the event the relationship is terminated.[13]

> In many states, if the franchisee is an agent the franchisor may be fined if he has failed to qualify to do business in the state.[14]

Most franchises contain a provision stating that the franchisee is not to act as an agent for the franchisor. Unfortunately, the authorities are in disagreement as to how far such a clause goes in deciding this crucial issue. A large part of the confusion here may be attributed to the fact that many franchisees do not logically fit into either the agency or independent-vendee categories. Franchisees normally have more independence than agents but less independence than ordinary buyers on the open market.

Franchise agreements typically include other provisions which:

(a) give the franchisor the right to change list prices at any time,
(b) obligate the franchisor to buy back new inventory (and parts) still in stock in the event of termination of the franchise,
(c) provide that the franchise cannot be assigned (transferred or sold) by the franchisee without the franchisor's consent,
(d) protect the franchisor's property in his trademark, and
(e) provide that no promises or representations other than those contained in the written franchise can bind the franchisor unless in writing and signed by a designated officer of the franchisor.

FRANCHISE LITIGATION

In the past franchisees suing for wrongful termination have had very limited success probably in major part because it is contrary to the interest of franchisors to terminate franchisees other than those which have proved to be incompetent, lazy, or dishonest.[15] On the other hand, it is possible that a particular franchisee may be terminated "arbitrarily" or "unfairly" because of a refusal to go along with unreasonable or even illegal demands made by the franchisor. Sometimes the franchisor's interest in maintaining market share or production goals may result in unreasonable pressure on particular franchisees. Sometimes the franchisor may decide to take over and conduct direct marketing operations in a territory which has been cultivated by a franchisee with reasonable expectations that the franchisee would have a reasonable time for recouping a large investment. Sometimes personality conflicts between franchisor sales representatives and individual franchisees may lead to friction and precipitous terminations.

Three developments which have improved franchisee litigation odds are: 1) adoption of the U.C.C.; 2) rapid growth of suits based on the antitrust laws; and 3) the development of franchisee-protective legislation and case decisions at the state level.

TERMINATION OF FRANCHISES UNDER THE U.C.C.

There are several sections of the U.C.C. which may be relevant to franchise terminations where the relationship involves sales of goods. In addition, some U.C.C. legal concepts have been applied by analogy to franchise relationships not involving "pure" sales of goods transactions.[16]

Sec. 1-102(3) provides that the provisions of the Code may be varied by agreement and to this extent suggests a traditional contractual approach to franchises. The latter part of this section, however, provides that obligations of good faith, diligence, and reasonableness prescribed in the Code "may not be disclaimed but the parties may by agreement determine the standards by which the performance of such obligations is to be measured if such standards are not manifestly unreasonable." The impact of this latter part on the law of franchises is not yet clear, but it appears that reasonable and objective standards should be drafted by franchisors as a basis for judging the performance of their franchisees.

Sec. 2-303 of the U.C.C. preserves the rights of the parties to a sale of goods contract to allocate their respective risks and burdens by agreement. These allocation rights, however, are made subject to Sec. 2-302 which authorizes the court to strike down any part of a sales contract found to be "unconscionable." A contract can be unconscionable in the eyes of the court if found to be "unfair" or "oppressive" — particularly if the agreement was "dictated" or offered on a take-it-or-leave-it basis by a dominant party (franchisor) to a weaker party (franchisee).

The entire thrust of the Code tends to make open, flexible business arrangements such as those created by most franchises more enforceable as contracts.[17] Sec. 2-204(3) sets the tenor by providing, even though one or more terms are left open, a contract of sale does not fail for indefiniteness if the parties intended to make a contract and there is a "reasonably certain basis for giving an appropriate remedy."

Sec. 2-309(2) and (3) are the only parts of the Code which specifically treat termination rights and liabilities. Subsec. (2) states that where a contract "provides for successive performances but is indefinite in duration it is valid for a reasonable time but unless otherwise agreed may be terminated at any time by either party." Subsec. (3) provides that "termination of a contract by one party except on the happening of an agreed event requires that reasonable notification be received by the other party and any agreement dispensing with notification is invalid if its operation would be unconscionable." Despite these specific provisions relating to termination, nearly all of the important franchise termination litigation in the state courts has developed out of special state legislation and out of the "good faith" and "unconscionability" concepts discussed previously.

STATE LEGISLATION AND DECISIONS

At least 22 states now have laws protecting various types of franchisees from terminations except "for good cause."[18] Under these statutes the burden of proving good cause is usually placed on the franchisor, with the courts looking unfavorably upon termination grounds based upon the franchisee's failure to comply with any franchisor demands the courts view as unreasonable.

In *Shell Oil Co. v. Marinello*, Shell Oil Co. brought suit to evict Marinello, a retail lessee-dealer.[19] Marinello commenced an action, which was consolidated with the oil company's action, for an injunction against the termination of his lease agreement and product franchise and for other equitable remedies. The court said:

> Surely no person would make the kind of investment in money, time and effort as did Marinello without the reasonable expectation that if he substantially performed his obligations to Shell, the latter would in turn continue to renew his lease and dealership. He was, by virtue of Shell's dominant position in their relationship and the legal structure of the agreements whose terms he could not vary, compelled to rely upon Shell's good faith in living up to these expectations.[20]

Consequently, the court held that as between these parties the lease and the dealer agreement are subject to the implied covenant that Shell would renew the agreements so long as defendant substantially performed his obligations to Shell.

Other courts have implied the "good faith" or "good cause" termination condition into various franchises.[21] The trend here as in other areas of the law is to protect the weak from the strong. Indeed, there may be serious antitrust implications if the court finds the franchisor has exercised coercion in any form against the franchisee. A franchisor's threat to terminate which causes a franchisee to maintain or raise a price is the equivalent of illegal price-fixing by the franchisor. A franchisor terminated a franchisee for the latter's refusal to accept a consignment contract. The franchisor was held liable for treble damages under the antitrust laws where the purpose of the coercive consignment plan was to stablize retail prices.[22]

CONCLUSION

It is clear that franchisors must now exercise careful draftmanship if they are to minimize the legal risks associated with franchising. Given the legal trends favoring franchisees, franchisors might consider adopting counter-strategies. The franchise could be drawn with at least the appearance of reasonableness and fairness after consideration is given to the franchisee's investment, the level of risks, and the reasonable expectations created at the time the franchise is signed. To lessen the appearance of unilateral dictation of terms, alternative terms or even alternative franchises of differing durations and risk patterns might be offered. Franchisees would then choose voluntarily among alternatives.

The grounds for termination should be clearly stated with appropriate fair notice and review procedures. The GM franchise obligates GM to buy back new models and parts and gives the cancelled GM dealer many other post termination aids.

It now appears that Berle was right when he wrote in 1954:

> One would expect to find a trend toward limitation on arbitrary power gradually appearing through the entire field — whether it concerns franchises granted by Coca Cola to a manufacturer-salesman, or dealer-company relationships prevailing between farm machinery companies and their outlets, or other like arrangements through the entire range.[23]

Reasonable terms and alternative terms or even a choice among different types of franchises might be offered to franchisees to lessen the chances that judges might find that the terms were "dictated" and, therefore, unconscionable. Fair termination procedures should be adopted with specified reasonable grounds for termination clearly stated in the franchise. As a guard against a charge of "bad faith", a franchisor should make an effort to give the franchisee reasonable notice of his shortcomings and an opportunity to correct them. Lastly, the possible antitrust implications of the relationship must be observed at all times.

ENDNOTES

1. "Franchise Outlet Sales in U.S. Are Expected to Grow 13% in 1978," *Wall Street Journal,* February 2, 1978, p. 1.
2. Management Control Potentials and Practices of Franchise Systems, Unpublished thesis, S. Michael Ingraham, University California at Los Angeles.
3. "Franchising Finds Its Industry," *Business Week,* June 19, 1965, p. 72.
4. U.S. v. Arnold Schwinn & Co., 388 U.S. 365 (1967).
5. See Michael B. Metzger, "Schwinn's Swan Song," *Business Horizons,* April 1978, p. 52.
6. Standard Oil of California v. U.S., 377 U.S. 293 (1949).
7. Siegel v. Chicken Delight, Inc., 448 F.2d 43 (9th Cir. 1971).
8. Susser v. Carvel Corporation, 332 F.2d 505 (2nd Cir. 1964) *cert. dismissed,* 381 U.S. 125 (1965), 42, 353.
9. See Gellhorn, "Limitations on Contract Termination Rights — Franchise Cancellations, 1967 **Duke L.J.**, 465.

10. A classic case on this is Joslyn v. Cadillac Automobile Co., 177 F, 863 (8th Cir. 1910).
11. Federal social security taxes, chain store taxes, and workmen's compensation laws could be involved, as well as union difficulties. See Hudspeth v. Esso Standard Oil, 170 F.2d 418 (8th Cir. 1948).
12. See "Note," 27 **Ind. L.J.** 524 (1952). It has been settled that manufacturers or suppliers have no right to control the resale prices of "independent" dealers.
13. A manufacturer generally owes his agent the legal duty of reimbursing the latter for all reasonable expenditures incurred in carrying out the manufacturer's business. In addition, at least some courts rule that a selling agent has stronger legal rights under a franchise than does an independent dealer.
14. If a manufacturer has selling agents in a state, state law usually requires that the manufacturer register to do business in the state. See Mario Florio, et. al., v. Powder-Power Tool Corp., 148 F. Supp., 843 (E.D., Pa.; 1956), and Eclipse Fuel Engineering Company v. Superior Court of the State of California, 307 P., 2d, 739 (Cal. 1957).
15. See Charles M. Hewitt, *Good Faith or Unconscionability — Franchisee Remedies for Termination,* 29 **Bus. Law** 227 (1973).
16. See Weaver v. American Oil Co., 276 N.E.2d 144 (1971).
17. See Warrick Beverage Corp. v. Miller Brewing Co., 352 N.E.2d 496 (Ct. App. Ind. 1976).
18. Note *Constitutional Obstacles to State 'Good Cause' Restrictions on Franchise Terminations,* 74 **Col. L. Rev.** 1487.
19. 120 N.J. Super. 357, 294 A.2d 253 (1972); aff'd, 307 A.2d 598 (N.J. Sup. Ct., 1973).
20. *Id.* 294 A.2d at 262.
21. Note *A Sui Generis Approach to Franchise Terminations,* 50 **Notre Dame Law** 545 (1975).
22. Simpson v. Union Oil Co. of California, 377 U.S. 13 (1964).
23. **Adolph A. Berle, Jr., The 20th Century Capitalistic Revolution** (New York; Harcourt, Brace & Co. 1954), 81.